Masters
Memories

Masters
Memories

⊷⊨ ○ ○ ○ ⊨⊶

by
CAL BROWN

SLEEPING BEAR PRESS
Chelsea, Michigan

Sleeping Bear Press
121 South Main
P.O. Box 20
Chelsea, MI 48118
www.sleepingbearpress.com

A few of these stories appeared in slightly different form in *Great Shots*, by Robert Sommers and Cal Brown, 1989, Chartwell Books, U.S.A., and Anaya, Great Britain. The stories of Gene Sarazen's double-eagle and the adventures of Jock Hutchison and Freddie McLeod were published originally in *Golf Digest*, and appear with some modifications with the kind permission of its Editor.

Printed and bound in Canada.

10 9 8 7 6 5 4 3 2

Library of Congress Cataloging-in-Publication Data

Brown, Cal.
    Masters memories / by Cal Brown.
        p. cm.
    ISBN 1-886947-46-5
    1. Masters Golf Tournament—History. 2. Augusta National Golf
Club—History. 3. Golfers. I. Title.
GV970.B74 1998
796.352'66—dc21   98-30971
                                                        CIP

Acknowledgments

Special thanks go to Dave Marr, who left us too soon, for his rich store of yarns, and to Byron Nelson, Billy Joe Patton, Gene Sarazen, Ed Sneed, Paul Runyan, and Ben Crenshaw for their detailed recollections. The author thanks Frank Christian, the official club photographer, for permission to include one or two stories; Mary Ellen Moore for editorial suggestions; and Al Ludwick for his yeoman research in the back issues of the *Augusta Chronicle* and *Augusta Herald*. And, to Brian Lewis, sincere thanks for his continuing interest in the lore of the game and in publishing it to a wide audience. This book is for Betsy and John Hemphill.

Preface

These tales are all true. Like most true stories, they represent the collected memories of witnesses and testimony from the perpetrators—which is to say, some facts and a few lies. The recollections include many from the principal figures featured in the Masters and the stories themselves, from Jones to Coe to Kuchar, from Sarazen to Nicklaus to Tiger Woods. The cast of characters includes Byron Nelson, Paul Runyan, Sam Snead, Ken Venturi, Ben Crenshaw, Billy Joe Patton, Ben Hogan, Harvie Ward, Ed Sneed, and many others whose recollections are woven into the stories, representing eventful moments from the first sixty-five years of the Masters Tournament.

A few, like Patton, Sneed, and Venturi didn't win the tournament, but their stories are part of the lore of the Masters and are explored. Some are about winning, others about being there. This is a miscellany, of course, but all of the stories are, in the end, about the creation of a golf course—the stage—the characters who are drawn to it—the players—and the renewal of a tournament—the play—that, year after year, produce for its audience more satisfying moments and high drama than just about any other in golf.

Contents

MASTERS MEMORIES

The Favorites

—⚬ ⚬ ⚬ ⚬ ⚬—

When the country's best professional and amateur golfers gathered in Augusta, Georgia, in March of 1934 for the first "Masters" tournament, the betting favorites were Bobby Jones, an amateur and the sentimental choice, and Paul Runyan, a professional and the season's leading money winner. Jones's friend and chronicler, O.B. Keeler, wrote in Wednesday's newspaper that week that Runyan "was playing simply colossal golf. I honestly believe his game around the green is the finest I ever beheld."

That year, Runyan and Craig Wood—the fellow Sarazen would catch and beat a year later in the second Masters—met in the finals of the PGA Championship. The two were level after thirty-six holes—Wood, one of the longest hitters in golf, and Runyan, one of the shortest. On the first extra hole, a 535-yard par-five, Wood whistled his second shot nine feet from the hole. Runyan, forty yards short of the green in two, knocked his approach dead, and Wood missed his putt. They halved in fours, but Wood, who had watched this sort of thing all day, was done. Runyan won on the next hole.

It was this style of play—popgun tee shots, followed by deadly fairway woods, and even deadlier chipping and putting—that wore down opponents and earned Runyan the nickname, Little Poison. He was cocky, feisty, and very good. He adored match play, where he knew his style would invariably exasperate his longer hitting (and who was not?) opponents. Over his career, in head-to-head matches with Craig Wood, Byron Nelson, Walter Hagen, Jug McSpaden, Sam Snead, Ben Hogan, and Gene Sarazen, Runyan won ten and lost just one—to Sarazen, with whom he was one and one, lifetime.

This was the man picked by the press as cofavorite, with Jones, when the fans gathered for that first Augusta National Invitational, as it was officially named. It was not much of a gathering by today's standards. "No one took it too seriously," recalled Runyan. "There were no more than four to five thousand people in the gallery the final day. The public had access to the clubhouse then, and the hosts were offering 'white lightning' to visitors. I think they had about fifty gallons to start with, but ran out the third day and had to order another fifty gallons."

In practice rounds, which began ten days before the tournament, Jones teamed with Ed Dudley, the host professional, against Runyan and his frequent partner, Horton Smith, another putting wizard. These were the two hottest players in golf at the time. "Jones was shooting fantastic rounds in practice," said Runyan, "turning in cards of 67s and 68s, and one 65. We managed to beat them once, though."

The Augusta National held a Calcutta pool, popular then but now illegal, in which players were auctioned off to the highest bidders at pari-mutuel odds. Runyan, the leading money winner on tour that winter, went for eighteen hundred dollars. Jones went for fourteen *thousand*.

However, Jones was having fits on the greens. The great man was hitting his woods as well as he ever had, his irons only slightly less so, but as the week wore on his putting deteriorated. On Wednesday's last practice round, he missed several putts, including one of eighteen inches at the last green, and spent much of the afternoon accepting putting lessons from two veterans O.B. Keeler described as "Dr. Bobby Cruickshank and Dr. Willie MacFarlane. They were engaged in a consultation of such portentous gravity that it seemed more like an autopsy." Prophetic words.

The favorites were paired the first two rounds, Runyan scoring 74-71 and Jones 76-74. During the first round, Jones hit a shot Runyan will never forget. They were at the long, downhill eleventh, the par-five that is now the second hole. "Jones drove beautifully down the fairway, and then hit a brassie—an old, traditional name for a two-wood—from a steep downslope," said Runyan. "The ball went up high and hung there for a while before it landed nine feet from the hole. It was a magnificent stroke. I hit a brassie second with everything I had, and couldn't reach the green."

The leader at the halfway point was Horton Smith, who shot 70-72, one stroke better than Ed Dudley. Smith went on to win, finishing the tournament at four-under-par 284, a stroke ahead of Craig Wood. In third place was Runyan, who shot the last three rounds in four-under—including a fatal seven after he hit two balls in the water at the thirteenth (then the fourth) hole in the final round—and tied at 286 with Billy Burke, the man who had succeeded Jones as U.S. Open champion in 1931.

Runyan continued to play in the Masters until 1942, when he again finished third, this time behind Byron Nelson and Ben Hogan (who went on to an historic playoff, won by Nelson). Paul Runyan returned to Augusta in his early fifties and played in three more Masters from 1958 to 1960, then retired. "The Masters was a product of two remarkable people, Bob Jones and Cliff Roberts," said Runyan. "They had a vision, and made it come true. Jones had the magnetism to give it heart, and Cliff had the organizational and business skills to make it work."

Runyan once worked for Spalding, as did Jones, and frequently traveled to Atlanta to promote the company's golf products. These trips continued for years, during which Paul often stopped to see his old colleague. "These visits were among the true delights of my life. The last time I saw him, Jones weighed not much more than a hundred pounds, but his mind was clear as a bell," said Runyan.

"Jones would invite me to his law office and we'd talk about his plans and hopes for the tournament. He wanted a place where his closest friends could come together to share memories and friendship. He hoped to create one of the best golf tournaments in the world, and I think everyone knows how well he and Cliff succeeded."

The Comet of '34

⊷═◐ ○ ○ ○ ◑═⊷

In the first Augusta National Invitational, Emmett French, a fine player from Southern Pines, North Carolina, fired a 70 in the opening round and shared the lead with veteran tour pros Horton Smith and Jimmy Hines. Horton Smith would go on to win that inaugural event, and Hines would tie for seventh with three others.

Smith and Hines should be recognized names today, although Smith is probably best known as the first Masters winner. He was a terrific putter, perhaps one of the best who ever lived, who won eight tournaments in one season on the professional tour, thirty-two in his career. Hines had less success, perhaps, but was a big hitter who had won both the Los Angeles and Metropolitan Opens, important tournaments in those days, and was a member of the 1939 Ryder Cup team.

Emmett French was a Pennsylvanian and an old U.S. Open hand who began playing in the national championship in 1915 when he finished in a tie for tenth with seven others, including Walter Hagen. He was a compatriot of Fred Brand, another western Pennsylvania pro, whose son, Fred, Jr., would later be-

⊷═◐ 5 ◑═⊷

come a member of the Augusta National Golf Club. French had tied for fifth with Bobby Jones and Alex Smith in the 1921 U.S. Open, and had finished fourth in the 1927 U.S. Open at Oakmont, ahead of Jones.

His greatest day came in 1922, when he reached the finals of the PGA Championship at Oakmont. There he faced the phenomenal Gene Sarazen, who had burst onto the professional scene earlier that summer at age twenty by winning the U.S. Open at Skokie in Glencoe, Illinois, whipping the great Bobby Jones, Bill Mehlhorn, Walter Hagen, and a strong field. French had done very well in the early PGA Championships, reaching the quarterfinals twice and the semifinals once, where he was beaten each time by Long Jim Barnes.

Finally, he had escaped his nemesis to find another waiting. French was the veteran at Oakmont, and was in his home territory, but he did no better than Hagen or Mehlhorn had done at Skokie, losing to Gene, 4 and 3. Sarazen became the first man to win both national championships the same year, another of the many "firsts" he would establish.

"Good old Emmett French," as he was frequently described by golf writer O.B. Keeler, was a tall, personable man of gracious habits who possessed a stylish game that perhaps lacked only a touch of inner fire. By 1933, French had moved to Southern Pines, North Carolina, that lovely countryside near Pinehurst, where he hoped to spend the rest of his life. He was in the Augusta National tournament, as were many of the players, as a man whose game Bobby Jones respected and whose company he welcomed. It was something of a surprise, though, when he shared scoring honors with Smith and Hines the first day.

Unfortunately, the admirable French did not fare so well in the second round as his coleaders. He followed his opening round of 70 with one of 83, then withdrew midway through the third round after turning the front nine in forty strokes. Joining him on the sidelines, incidentally, were several current and future stars, including Wild Bill Mehlhorn, Dick Metz, Lighthorse Harry Cooper, future Ryder Cupper Herman Barron, and future U.S. Open champion Tony Manero, all of whom withdrew.

Emmett French never returned to the Masters. Perhaps he had seen what he came to see. His blazing start and finish in flames has almost, but never, quite been equaled. As so many of us have done, he held the unicorn for a day and awoke the next to touch it no more.

A Measure of Greatness

✦═◉ ○ ○ ○ ◉═✦

I f somehow Charles Coody were to catch lightning in a bottle again and win a second Masters title, or if Tommy Aaron were to do so, another of golf's tradition myths would crumble into dust. History casts no disrespect on Coody, Aaron, Herman Keiser, Claude Harmon, Larry Mize, or others whose lone major victory came at Augusta National.

In the two-thirds of a century since the Masters began, only thirteen men have won it twice or more. The redoutable Nicklaus has won six, and Palmer four, while Demaret, Snead, Player, and Faldo have each won three. The rest—Nelson, Hogan, Smith, Watson, Ballesteros, Langer, and, most recently, Crenshaw —have all won twice. While several players who would be included on a list of the all-time greats have won the Masters only once, among them Sarazen, Middlecoff, and Casper, the evidence to date suggests that no one wins the Masters a second or third time who is not a great player.

This has not been the case in the U.S. Open, which seems to

provide advantages to certain types of players who otherwise might be regarded as journeymen. A case in point is Andy North, who has won two U.S. Opens but only two other tour events. To win any U.S. Open is an achievement, and to win two is a monument of spirit and determination and composure, so to single out North can take nothing away from the man himself. But I'm reasonably certain that even North would not place himself in the ranks of golf's greatest players.

Of the multiple winners of the Masters, it might be argued that Horton Smith and Bernhard Langer belong in the same category because they did not win another of golf's major tournaments. If not quite a legend, Smith was certainly a legendary putter. Bernard Darwin wrote that his putting "was a joy to watch and of a horrid certainty." Smith was known as the Joplin Ghost, the "man with the velvet touch" on the greens, and, in the era following Hagen, Sarazen, and Armour, was the tour's most consistent winner with thirty-two victories. With Paul Runyan, another short game wizard who won twenty-nine PGA tournaments in his career, and Harry Cooper, who won everything except a major, and Denny Shute, the icy winner of three majors, Smith was one of a quartet of players who came to the fore in the late 1920s and dominated professional golf for nearly a decade before the arrival of Nelson, Snead, Demaret, Guldahl, Picard, and Hogan.

Like Runyan and Picard, Horton Smith won only two majors, but few would deny that these men were among the game's great players. Langer's claim is weakest of all, having won only three times in America, coupled with his failure, until now, to win the British Open. The resourceful German has won everything in Europe, where he spends most of his time, but until he wins the Open or establishes a better record on the American tour, his bona fides are weaker than the others. Still, he is reckoned among the world's best players today.

So, we are brought back to the point, if indeed there is one, that only great players have won two or more Masters, which leads us to the character and competitive strength of the Augusta National golf course. It has been said often enough that great players tend to win on great courses. Put another way, golf courses can be measured by the quality of the players who win there. Certainly there have been exceptions, but a glance at the roster of Masters winners shows how the great players have dominated the event:

Multiple Winners

Jack Nicklaus	6
Arnold Palmer	4
Jimmy Demaret	3
Sam Snead	3
Gary Player	3
Nick Faldo	3
Horton Smith	2
Byron Nelson	2
Ben Hogan	2
Tom Watson	2
Seve Ballesteros	2
Bernhard Langer	2
Ben Crenshaw	2

Perhaps this alone is not a validation of the strength of the Augusta National golf course, but it may indicate something about its character.

"Augusta National gives you plenty of rope to hang yourself," says Ben Crenshaw, the most recent of the multiple winners. "You have all this room out there, and still we manage to hit it off line. Every player has that little voice in his brain goading him on. You're tempted and dared to try a shot because of the design of the holes. On other courses we play, the hazards are immediately seen and obvious. At Augusta, some hazards are

obvious, but many are not apparent until you get up on them—
it might be a swale, a subtle angle—and this lulls you to sleep. It
creates confusion in your mind, and I think Bobby Jones and
Alister Mackenzie intended that we have this conflict between
the ears."

A colleague, Ed Sneed, underscores Crenshaw's views. "It
takes every bit of self-control not to go for it on those par-fives,"
said Sneed. "If the ball is in a good lie, and no trees intervene,
you know you can reach the green. It's really hard to resist, because it's against all your instincts to do so." We can imagine
that that's exactly what Mackenzie and Jones had in mind, or
are we giving them too much credit, after all?

From the beginning, the Augusta National course was recognized as more than a pretty face. The pros in 1934 praised
Mackenzie's work, and the writers provided a chorus of assent.
O.B. Keeler caught it just about right, though somewhat floridly,
when he wrote: "The Augusta National, bland and brilliant and
tender as a cluster of emeralds on the white brow of a movie
queen, can strike back with the lash of a Jack Dempsey at someone taking undue liberties, or missing untoward shots. The good
Dr. Mackenzie, with all his kindliness, arranged it that way. The
boys wanting to score will surely find the occasional grim and
perplexing problem in their paths."

That part hasn't changed at all, for even though the course
has undergone many changes over the years, its heart has not.
"Augusta National is a mental course, and extremely emotional,
too," Crenshaw goes on. "It's an emotional roller-coaster because of the temptations it offers, and because you almost have
to dare yourself to hit certain shots. It's fascinating that this
course came from the most cerebral golfer in history. The rout-
ing is certainly Alister Mackenzie; he had a way of taking property to the bank. The thought process, though, has a lot of Jones
in it."

Does this explain why Augusta National is such an elusive

measure of golfing temper and ability? Is it finally this that leads to all those dramatic finishes on Sunday at the Masters? What it may suggest is that Jones and Mackenzie understood, better than the United States Golf Association does, the compelling influence of risk vs. reward in a great championship. Give these great players a chance for everything, and some will seize it. Or, in the attempt, some may fail, and that is what brings such an edge to the drama at the Masters. Dangle temptation in front of a man for three rounds, and he may finally, as Ed Sneed suggests, be unable to resist even when he knows he must.

So, which is it to be? Does the golf course measure the quality and character of its winners, or is it the other way around?

A Nightmare and a Dream

The traditions that have grown up around the Masters are more than the dusty memories of old Freddie McLeods and Gene Sarazens, and the sturdy legends of Snead and Demaret and Palmer. These have to do with the Augusta National golf course itself, of how its holes are shaped and how they are laid into the contours of the land.

Alister Mackenzie and Bob Jones, the designers of the Augusta National, knew a thing or two about the game. They understood the situations that compel a great player to bring all his capacities to bear and they seem to have shared an instinct for the features most likely to inspire, indeed to incite the critical moment. If they were after drama, they succeeded, probably more than they dreamed they might.

These great moments have occurred most often on the second nine of this now-historic golf course, a glorious stretch of holes which puts forth temptation in its most beautiful guise and then exposes a man's weakness, be it his composure, his judgment, or his courage.

Surely no one appreciates this more than Ben Crenshaw, who has such a keen interest in the history and traditions of the game, and who had always yearned to win at Augusta. Those who watched his performance there and found him such a sympathetic character felt it was only a matter of time before he won. Popular sentiment seldom enters into the equation at the Masters, but when Crenshaw's time came, as it did in 1984, there could not have been a single witness who did not feel a sense of approval and satisfaction.

Crenshaw's flaw is width, rather than length, which led Tom Weiskopf to quip, "Ben is the only top professional who gets the yips with his driver." Ben has admitted that his drives "put me in more precarious positions than anyone," but that week his adventurous swing was under control and he was, as he usually was, holing out from everywhere with the most envied putting stroke in the game. Ben climbed into the lead after birdies at the eighth and ninth holes in the final round, but he knew the real test was to come. Gil Morgan and David Edwards had mounted a late rush, and Tom Watson was closing in.

The players believe, with justification, that the Masters begins only when they reach those final nine holes on Sunday; until then, says tournament lore, they have only been jockeying for position. There, at the majestic tenth, Crenshaw holed a preposterous putt of nearly seventy feet. "It was absolutely off the charts," said Ben. "After it went in, I began to think it might be my day." For mortals, the putt of a lifetime, but an even better one was to come.

A cautious bogey at the eleventh, a brave birdie at the dreaded twelfth and then a careful par at the thirteenth. A poor tee shot at the fourteenth put him behind some trees, forcing Ben to play a hooked approach that came off well enough but carried too far and stayed on top of the viciously contoured green. The fourteenth green is a horrid business that must be seen to appreciate what Crenshaw now faced. His ball lay ninety feet from the hole and would have to run severely downhill across a bewildering array of humps and mounds.

Even for a putter of Crenshaw's reputation, the odds favored his putting the ball off the green. Ever so delicately he stroked his ball—and the putt died eighteen feet short of the hole. Now he looked at another downhill horror, but this one would break sharply, and more than once. Only a holed putt, he felt, could stop the ball from rolling past the cup. If he missed, Crenshaw thought to himself, a six was not out of the question and his advantage would be gone.

He could sense the tournament balanced on the treacherous slopes before him. "It was a devil of a putt, but I could see what I had to do. I knew this was the critical stroke," Crenshaw said. Another careful glance at the line and the putt was away. It broke left, ran across a little shelf, then over a soft hump and, just before it died, gathered speed, swerved hard left and dived into the hole. He had done it.

Crenshaw finished with a 68 and a total of 277, two strokes ahead of Watson. Asked to compare the two long putts he had holed at the tenth and fourteenth, Ben smiled and said: "The putt at fourteen was a nightmare. The other one was a dream." For Crenshaw, and the Masters Tournament, another dream come true.

Hogan's Lament

❖⇒○ ○ ○ ⇐❖

It was Ben Hogan's lot to show nothing when he played, to allow no emotion to escape his countenance while competing. He had learned at an early age to bury his emotions deep, to channel them into the shape and movements of his golf swing. Though not at first, he became the best of his kind, the man who could control golf shots and the game they described better than anyone alive.

At first glance, Hogan appeared small; he was no more than 5-foot-8, but his hands were huge and his forearms the shape of a blacksmith's. "I saw him undressed once in the locker room, and his legs and buttocks were like a fullback's, very powerful," said Dave Marr. "I was surprised, to be honest, but look at how far he hit the ball. When he needed distance, it was always there."

There were photographs of Hogan smiling, but never on the golf course. Always, they were captured in awards ceremonies or during unguarded moments while he relaxed in the clubhouse. No one needed to be told that golf was anything but serious business to Hogan; it was written in his face. Golf was not life and death, but it was pretty close, his expression said.

Somehow Ben Hogan's journey took him through a bleak childhood, ten years of golfing misery, three failed attempts to make the pro tour, a head-on collision with a bus and a remade golf swing, to a glorious but relatively short reign at the pinnacle of golf, then a bitter case of the putting yips and an unceremonious exit from the 1957 Masters. For the first time that year, the tournament was cut after two rounds to the low forty and ties, a policy instituted because the field had grown substantially in the postwar years.

This sent two of the favorites, Hogan and Cary Middlecoff, to the sidelines along with other stars Mike Souchak, Tommy Bolt, Bob Toski, Gene Littler, and Bob Rosburg. It was in the locker room after the cut that Hogan made his infamous suggestion that putting be eliminated from the game. "I've always contended that golf is one game, and putting is another," Hogan told the press. "If I had my way, every golf green would be made into a huge funnel; you hit the funnel, and the ball would roll down a pipe into the hole."

No holes, just funnels? Later, Hogan would modify his plan, eliminating both the funnel and the hole but retaining the flagsticks. Under the new plan, the player hitting closest to the flagstick wins, and guess who would win that game? He told the scribes that putting is the least important of golf's essentials; driving the most important. "Show me a player who depends on putting, and I'll show you a man who won't stand up to the steady grind of tournament golf," Hogan declared. He would learn otherwise.

Hogan's rounds of 76-75-151 had left him one stroke over the cut, which he blamed on poor putting. "I couldn't get the ball in the hole," he said, with disgust. "I had four three-putt greens each day, but my putting's been bad for four years." Four years earlier, Hogan had played the greatest golf of his life in winning his second Masters title. That year, he set a tournament record of 274, breaking the old one by five shots.

At the presentation, Hogan said: "I hope to come back next year and play the same caliber of golf." Byron Nelson, paired with Ben in the final round, grabbed the microphone and retorted: "If you do, you'll be playing here all by yourself," drawing chuckles from the gallery.

That was nothing new for Hogan, whose practice sessions were almost always conducted in solitude. His long journey in golf led, finally, to a secluded practice fairway at the Shady Oaks Country Club where he spent his remaining days hitting glorious shots and defying those detestable holes in the greens. On one such occasion, he was practicing for the Colonial National Invitation tournament, held at the Colonial Country Club in his home town of Fort Worth, an event Hogan won five times.

Watching was Herbert Warren Wind, master of the well-turned phrase, who had collaborated with Hogan on his classic instruction book, *Five Lessons: The Modern Fundamentals of Golf*. Herb would sometimes repeat this incident, which happened a decade before Ben Crenshaw won his first Masters, to his golfwriting colleagues. The youngster was a fledgling pro competing in the Colonial National and had gone over to Shady Oaks to practice, perhaps even hoping to find Hogan there.

Find him he did, and Crenshaw, being young and fearless, approached the great man on the practice range, and asked: "Hi, Mr. Hogan, how ya doing?" Hogan glanced up to identify the intruder, and responded softly: "Well, I'm only hitting it eighty percent. I'm not really warmed up yet."

Hogan continued to hit one perfect shot after another, working his way through the bag until he reached the driver. He was warm now, and began hitting rifle shots with the big stick. Each ball was launched with a sharp crack, penetrating the distance in a slow, rising parabola. After a dozen or so, he turned to Crenshaw and said: "Here, young fella, let me see what you can do with this club." He handed him the weapon, the stiffest in golf.

Crenshaw could barely lift it. The shaft was a telephone pole, stiff as an iron pike. He swung at a ball and dribbled it along the ground. The young man teed another, higher this time, and skipped it across the grass. He squirted another ball weakly off to the right. He couldn't get one airborne. Finally, Hogan took back the driver, and tossed a withering glance in Crenshaw's direction.

Silence for a moment, then Hogan asked: "Tell me, young man, what did you shoot today?"

"A 64," Crenshaw replied, brightly.

Hogan's shoulders slumped, his expression paled. Slowly, he shook his head.

Here was a youngster who drove it crooked, hit wild iron shots, and holed putts from every corner of the greens. What had the great man done to deserve this? You could almost hear the words stabbing through Hogan's brain: "Take that, Hogan! That'll teach you the value of putting! The shame of it!"

What could the great man do? Not a thing, not one damn thing. Not one. Damn. Thing.

A Famous Shot

⊷⇨ ○ ○ ○ ⇦⊷

The original "shot heard round the world" was sounded alongside a country lane near Concord, Massachusetts, and touched off the American Revolution. Another was fired in the little city of Sarajevo, killing an Archduke and providing the spark that touched off World War I. The third was appropriated by a sporting event in the little city of Augusta, Georgia, and, though not as fateful as the first two, brought worldwide recognition to a golf tournament and helped establish it as one of the game's classic events.

"When the wand touches him, Gene is likely to win in a great finish as he did at Fresh Meadow and Skokie, or in a parade as he did at Prince's; but if it touches him not, the boldness of his play leaves no middle ground. When he is in the right mood, he is probably the greatest scorer in the game, possibly that the game has ever seen." Bobby Jones wrote these words in 1932 to describe his fearless contemporary, Gene Sarazen. Three years later Jones would stand on the golf course he built in Augusta, Georgia, and watch Sarazen fire that famous golf shot.

Sarazen holed a four-wood second shot on the par-five fifteenth in the final round at the Augusta National and went on to win the second Masters Tournament played. If not the greatest, that shot is certainly the most famous single stroke in the history of American golf. Sarazen's double-eagle dramatized, as no other shot had done, that rare achievement, scoring three under par on a given hole.

Gene had broken all the windows in practice that week, touring four rounds in 271 strokes. That 72-hole score, seventeen under par, would not be matched for thirty years, and then only by the mighty Nicklaus. The stunning exhibition might have been an omen, but by the time Sarazen reached the fifteenth tee on Sunday, the 1935 Masters seemed to be over, with Craig Wood the certain winner.

Wood had birdied the final hole and posted a score of 282. Sarazen would have to birdie three holes to tie. Besides, the club already had made out the winner's check to Wood, who was accepting congratulations in the clubhouse, although Cliff Roberts later denied it, claiming it was done "only for photographic purposes," whatever those were.

The fifteenth measured 485 yards that day, a straightaway hole with a pond in front of the green. The hole has been lengthened to 520 yards, and the pond broadened from its original width of thirty feet to about fifty feet, but even then, a player thought twice before going for the green with his second shot. The turf was firmer than it is now, and Sarazen's drive, aided by a slight draw, had rolled to a stop in the center of the fairway about 255 yards from the tee.

No more than twenty-five people huddled near the green on that blustery April afternoon; most of the gallery had flocked to the eighteenth to watch Craig Wood. "I've met about twenty thousand people who claim they saw the shot," Sarazen recalled. Two who did were Walter Hagen, with whom Gene was paired, and Bobby Jones, who was perched on one of the large mounds between the fifteenth and seventeenth fairways.

Jones was enjoying the role of spectator after a brief fling in the second round. Following an opening round of 74, Bobby started fast the next morning, firing a 33 on the front nine. Word spread that "Jones was back." But he lost his touch on the homeward nine, giving back the three strokes to par and putting himself somewhere in the middle of the pack. Sitting in the clubhouse afterward, he told sports writers: "Maybe I'm just a nine hole golfer."

Now, having finished his final round, Jones waited at the fifteenth to watch Hagen and Sarazen finish. It was a little past 5:30 on Sunday afternoon. A roar from the eighteenth green, whipped by a cold gust of wind, reached them, followed moments later by the news of Wood's birdie. As Sarazen reached his ball, Hagen shook his head and called over: "Well, that's that," implying the tournament was all over.

"Oh, I don't know," Sarazen replied, more to himself than to his impatient playing partner, "they might go in from anywhere." As Sarazen pondered the shot, Hagen hollered across the fairway: "Hey, hurry up, Gene, I've got a date tonight."

Gene's ball was sitting down in the grass. He turned to his caddie, an amiable, lanky man called Stovepipe: "I'm going for it," Sarazen announced. "What do I need?" Stovepipe's glance darted between ball and target: "Mister Gene," he drawled, "you gots to hit you a three-wood if you wants to clear that water."

"I don't want the three-wood," Sarazen said finally, and pulled out his four-wood. He toed in the face, took his stance and swung. The ball rose about forty feet, flew dead straight, and landed a few inches short of the green. "I hit it pure," Gene said later. "All I was hoping to do was make a four."

Bob Jones watched as the ball skipped low onto the putting surface and ran toward the flagstick, set in the right rear of the green about fifteen feet from the back edge. "My God," Jones thought, "he's going to have a chance at a three." An instant later the ball rolled up and in. Later, the shot was paced off at 232 yards.

"The first thing I thought about was what I would have to do on the last three holes to tie Wood," Sarazen said. "I felt no elation. It came too quick." On the last three holes, Jones remembered that Gene left himself difficult putts for pars and made them all. "What impressed me most was his absolute confidence," said Jones. "He walked right up and struck them solidly and quickly. Every one went into the center of the hole. Gene was one of those players who, when he got on a hot streak, charged around the course like a tiger."

After making the double-eagle, Sarazen never doubted he would tie Wood and then win the playoff, which, for the only time in its history, was thirty-six holes. The next day, Gene shot 144 against Wood's 149. A bridge was erected across the pond in 1955 and named for Sarazen, in honor of the historic stroke.

Sarazen is probably remembered as much for this feat as for being the first to collect the winner's trophies at the U.S. Open, the British Open, the PGA and the Masters during his career, the so-called professional slam, or for having won the U.S. Open at the age of twenty, or for his remarkable longevity. Any of these achievements would place him in the record books, and, together, among golf's immortals.

Many years later, he reminisced about the double-eagle from his home in Marco Island, Florida. "You know, that was a lucky shot. It meant so much at the time, but I'm almost getting tired of hearing about it." Gene Sarazen was never a man to look back on things, but you can be sure that whenever the subject turns to golf's dramatic strokes, Sarazen's is one of the first to be mentioned. Gene was no stranger to historic occasions, and if he eventually grew tired of recalling this one, history has not.

A Home for
Double-Eagles

◦━━━◦ ○ ○ ○ ◦━━━◦

G ene Sarazen's famous double-eagle in 1935 did much to put
the Masters Tournament on the map, but he's not the only
man to hole the par-five fifteenth in two. In fact, at least five
others have done so, and perhaps more. The Augusta National
has an unwritten but strictly enforced rule that members' exploits will not see the light of day. The proscription against public celebration of members' exploits was instituted by Clifford
Roberts, who ran the club in an autocratic style for forty years
and who established most of its rules in order to safeguard the
privacy of its members.

Ordinarily, we would do nothing to disturb this sense of
decorum, but it's pretty hard to stop the ripples, as inevitable
as they are gentle, from the most famous shot in golf history.
In 1985, the fiftieth anniversary of Sarazen's historic deuce,
an amateur named W. Duff McCready duplicated The Squire's
feat. Playing from the members' tees, which shortens the hole
to about 480 yards, McCready cracked a fine tee shot that

traveled far enough to tempt him to go for the green. Some time later, the distance to the cup was measured at 218 yards. McCready, a five-handicapper from Pittsburgh, chose a Ginty, a lofted wood designed to escape from trouble, because he wanted "to hit the ball high in order to hold the green." Hold it he would, and holed it he did. His ball cleared the pond in front of the green and, like Sarazen's fifty years earlier, bounced onto the green and vanished into the hole.

These were not the only double-eagles recorded at this enchanting par-five, created by the marvelous collaboration between golf architect Alister Mackenzie and Augusta National founder Bobby Jones. In the mid-1960s, a former assistant pro at the club named Dave Hill—who is no relation to the touring pro of the same name—made his own double-eagle here, and in 1964, the brilliant amateur, Charlie Coe, who is a member of the Augusta National, recorded yet another at the fifteenth.

The parade continued in November of 1991 when Charles Morris, of Savannah, the owner of a chain of newspapers and radio stations and another member of the club, holed a three-wood second at the fifteenth to become the fifth man to emulate Sarazen's feat. (Three months later, incidentally, in early 1992, Morris scored yet another double-eagle, this one at the uphill eighth hole, again with a three-wood second. This feat duplicated Bruce Devlin's deuce scored at the same hole in the 1967 Masters.) Thirty years later, during an outing held for the volunteers who served at the 1997 Masters, Augusta resident J. Grice Keel became the most recent golfer to record a double-eagle at the fifteenth.

Because of the club's policy of secrecy, one can't be sure that this is a complete accounting of the lucky strokes that have fallen at this adventuresome par-five. One thing is certain, though; rather than suggesting that the hole is too easy, these incidents show why it is such an intriguing and, for all of its danger, promising call to those reckless impulses the game so obligingly indulges us.

Arnie's Place

⊶⟾ ∘ ∘ ∘ ⟽⊷

Gene Wojciechowski, a reporter for the *Chicago Tribune*, not long ago offered an opinion that "the two hardest things in sports are carrying four cups of beer in two hands, and making a downhill four-footer at Augusta National's sixteenth green." Well, Gene, no thirsty sportsman would dispute the first claim; as for the second, let me introduce you to Arnold Daniel Palmer.

Before proceeding, it is understood that certain fellows own certain golf courses. The Colonial in Fort Worth was Hogan's, whether you called it an Alley or not. Snead absolutely owned the Greensboro courses. Pebble Beach belonged to Mark O'Meara (and still does, for all we know), and the Augusta National is and always will be Palmer's private garden party—never mind those six jackets won by Nicklaus. It was here the Army was born in 1958, and here that Arnie performed several hundred miracles, stopping short only of walking on water which, among mortals, was the sole province of former Augusta National chairman Clifford Roberts.

Almost from the beginning of his appearances there, the

Masters galleries made Palmer their own. He had shown he might do anything, and they grew to expect it of him. Roars would accompany his slightest effort, and reverberant groans his heroic failures. Arnold's attacking style, of course, was not developed at the Masters. He did it everywhere, but it was magnified at Augusta National, the kind of golf course where risks are offered at every turn and are designed to be accepted. The place fit him like a glove—it was his kind of course, and these fans his kind of people.

In 1962, Arnold was hitching and puffing his way to what he hoped would be his third Masters title. He had scorched the first three rounds in eleven under par, two strokes ahead of a close friend, Dow Finsterwald, and four better than an old rival, Gary Player. In Dave Marr's words, "Arnold was breaking all the china in the shop," and had begun talking about beating Hogan's tournament record of 274. Reaching the sixteenth hole on Sunday, however, Palmer trailed this formidable pair by two shots. All three men were reckoned superb clutch putters by their peers, and it was putting that almost surely would, as it so often did, decide matters here.

The sixteenth is one of the most beautiful par-threes in golf, and possesses one of its most exasperating greens owing to its severe slopes and glassy surface. Men have putted in semicircles trying to follow the contours of this green. Fellows who own considerable reputations with a blade have taken four, even five putts to get down. On this Sunday, Palmer's tee shot was a bit strong and bounced into the fringe at the back right of the green. This left him with a downhill chip of some fifty feet.

The irrepressible Dave Marr had missed the cut that year, and was an interested spectator at sixteen. "Arnold was about to shoot 75, and he almost forgot to win the tournament," said Marr. "But that's what made him Arnold Palmer. You see, Jack Nicklaus never would have done that. With a lead like Arnold had, Jack would have slowly drowned those other two guys until there was nothing but bubbles. Meanwhile, Arnold might come out with blood all over him; he might win, but look like he lost."

Now Palmer needed at least a birdie, and maybe two, to have any chance. Surveying the situation for the radio audience, three-time Masters winner Jimmy Demaret softly murmured: "It looks as though he has no hope of holing this one." Palmer overheard him, and glared.

"You can't putt, let alone chip it close from where Arnold was, not unless your ball has Velcro on it" said Marr. "But, one thing Arnold never got credit for was his chipping and pitching; he was a wonderful chipper of the ball."

Beside the sixteenth green is one of those marvelous scoreboards for which the Masters Tournament is justly admired. The numbers are huge, all the better for spectators to read, and are manipulated from behind by eager young golfers. As Arnie prepared to play his delicate shot, the scoreboard correctly read, "Palmer, 6 under par." As he stood over the ball, the young man on the scoreboard dipped into his bin of numbers and hauled out a "7." He was observed by Dave Marr.

"Just as Arnold chipped, the scoreboard keeper started walking toward that '6' beside Palmer's name," Marr recalled. "Arnold's ball hit the green softly and rolled slowly toward the cup. You knew it was a good chip when he hit it, but before the ball reached the hole, the young man slapped that red '7' up on the scoreboard. And just about that time, the ball rolled into the hole. It was scary. Even today, you can't tell people that story without them looking at you funny. I still get chills thinking about it."

As it happened, Palmer and Marr were paired in the final round in 1964. This was to be the last of Arnold's four Masters victories, and the last major title he would win. Far behind at the start of the round, Marr had caught a hot streak and had crept to within three strokes after Palmer took three putts at the tenth green. Because of the arrangement of the tenth and eleventh holes, the caddies customarily wait at the edge of the tenth green to hand the players their drivers. The players then walk in one direction to the eleventh tee, while the caddies make their way through the forest in another direction to emerge far down the eleventh fairway in a position to forecaddie.

"As I went by my caddie to collect my driver," Marr reported, "I overheard Arnold's caddie, Ironman, ask in a clear voice: 'Boss, is you choking?' Well, I couldn't believe it, and I started to giggle. Arnold gave him one of those glares, and stormed up the path to the eleventh tee. He was mad; I could hear him whacking the bushes with his driver as went.

"Funny things get said on the golf course, but that's one of the most startling comments in a moment of intense pressure that I've ever heard. I couldn't help bursting out in laughter, but all it did was make Arnold play better. It turned out alright for him because I bogeyed the next two holes, falling into a tie with Nicklaus, and Arnold went on to win by six shots."

It was on the final hole of this tournament that the sharp-witted and sometimes dagger-tongued Marr uttered one of his famous retorts. Waiting on the eighteenth tee, Palmer turned to Marr and, undoubtedly thinking of the roaring galleries pressing in on all sides, inquired courteously if there were anything he could do to make the finish more comfortable for his playing partner. Without missing a beat, Marr quipped: "Yeah, make a 12."

Before he died in 1997, Dave Marr reminisced about Palmer's place in the game and in the history of the Masters. "Today, when Arnold appears in tournaments I sometimes hear guys question why he continues to play at, say, Augusta, or on the Senior Tour. It kinda makes me feel bad to hear players talk about him that way, and then I think to myself, 'why you stupid little man, he's the reason you're playing for all that money today.' Those guys ought to hit their knees every night and thank Arnold—for their jet, for their inflated endorsements, for the huge purses of today, and most of all for what he's given to the game and to all the players who have followed him."

The Big Blow
of '36

⊷≈⊙ ∘ ∘ ∘ ⊙≈⊶

When Gene Sarazen and Craig Wood resumed their Masters rivalry in 1936, they faced a tougher foe than each other. Torrential rains wiped out Thursday's opening round, so the tournament got underway on Friday in freezing temperatures and high winds. Sarazen, who won the famous playoff the previous year, shot 78, and Wood, his equal for four rounds, shot 88 that Friday.

The carnage was widespread; nineteen men failed to break 80, and half a dozen more were within a stroke of that figure. Jess Sweetser, former American and British amateur champ, "turned in 40 and came back an hour and a half later in 49," reported O.B. Keeler. "At that, I broke 90," Sweetser said cheerfully. Torchy Toda, with Chick Chin Augusta's first visiting Japanese players, each handed in an 81. "Wind go puff, puff. Oh, Oh. My, my. No good," lamented Torchy. Lighthorse Harry Cooper, reckoned by his peers the *original* best player who never won a major, fired a 70. "It was the best round of golf I ever played in my life," said Cooper, who followed with a round of 69 to no one's surprise, and held a commanding lead of five strokes after two days.

The last two rounds were scheduled for Sunday, but another downpour canceled Sunday's finale. The footbridge at twelve went under water, along with part of the thirteenth fairway, rendering the twelfth unplayable. The club considered using a rowboat to reach the twelfth green, or perhaps playing two other holes twice on Monday to avoid further postponement. Spectators arriving on buses Sunday were greeted with postponement signs, and a half dozen players pulled out of the tournament. "Maybe it's because we opened the course on Friday the thirteenth," was host Bob Jones's rueful comment.

Two rounds, then, on Monday in spite of horrible weather; the last round caught the tail end of a hurricane. Bob Jones finished with 77-306, thirty-two strokes higher than his practice rounds. "Try as hard as I can, I simply can't concentrate any more on my golf when the pressure is on," said Jones afterward. "When the old urge was with me, I could shut out everything else but my golf. Now I find myself repeatedly disconcerted by some stray conversation, the click of a camera, or movement in the gallery. I'm not able anymore to shut out the world and play the shots with the complete detachment that is vital in competition. Small things that I never noticed before now bother me and distract whatever attention I have left." It was the end of a comeback that had never been anything but halfhearted, a shadow passing across one of golf's most glorious careers.

The two delays unhinged Cooper, too. After a brave 71 Monday morning, he ballooned to 76 in the afternoon to finish a stroke behind Horton Smith, who picked up seven shots over those last two rounds. The weather was so bad, the pros petitioned in vain for another postponement. Smith had to chip across a flooded tenth green and made an heroic bogey, then played a truly miraculous stroke at the roller-coaster fourteenth when he chipped fifty feet across the green into the cup for birdie through the puddles and fog. He then claimed a spectacular par at the seventy-first hole when he ran a forty-foot putt seventeen feet past the cup, and holed coming back to claim his second Masters in three years.

Mother Nature had dumped nine inches of rain on the course in four days, and swept away the unlucky Cooper, with many others. Why it didn't treat the winner with equal contempt—nor Gene Sarazen, who posted the best round of the day, a lovely 70—is just another of those puzzles that bring mayhem and uncertainty to the final holes of nearly every Masters Tournament since Sarazen's fancy trick in the second one.

Bad weather had diminished the effect of the Masters, along with its gate receipts, once too often. Tournament chairman Clifford Roberts changed the dates of the 1937 event from late March to early April, which is where they remain.

The Great Playoff
of '42

✦⟫⟞○ ○ ○ ⟝⟪✦

When Byron Nelson came to the final hole of the 1942 Masters, you could almost feel it coming. Something dreadful or something wonderful was about to happen. Both, as it turned out. Nelson needed a four to tie Ben Hogan, who had been eight strokes behind after thirty-six holes, but now waited in the clubhouse with a score of 280. Only Nelson could catch him and everyone wanted to see a showdown between these two.

Although their greatest days still lay ahead of them, Nelson and Hogan, along with Snead, were the men their rivals feared most. Nelson had already won the U.S. Open, the PGA Championship, and the Masters. Hogan had yet to win one of those, but he had been the PGA's leading money-winner in 1940 and 1941.

Ben Hogan was a determined, implacable opponent, certain of his inner resources. Jimmy Demaret once said: "The only emotion Ben shows in defeat is surprise. You see, he expects to win." Within Byron Nelson burned a fierce, blinding rectitude that could not be stayed except by the man himself. The flame sometimes drove him to do things that could not be done.

One could not choose between them in the pure physical mastery of their shots. Hogan was longer, but Nelson was straighter. There was not a better long-iron player than Nelson, but Hogan was as good. Nelson would hole more crucial putts than anyone until Nicklaus came along, but who has been deadlier from ten feet in than Hogan? Both were scoring machines. When they made mistakes, it was news.

In practice rounds, Hogan had been in good form, shooting 68, although the hottest players were Jimmy Hines, Denny Shute, and Sam Byrd with 65s. Another player catching fire was Bobby Jones, paired with Nelson in a practice round against Henry Picard and Gene Sarazen. After a 38 on the front, Jones tore up the back in 31 strokes and teamed so well with his partner that Sarazen, catching a little flame himself and coming home with seven straight birdies, was unable to win a single hole.

In the first round, Byron Nelson and Paul Runyan shot matching 67s to set a terrific pace. Chatting with the press in the clubhouse, Byron wore a big grin: "I've discovered a secret about playing this course," he chortled. "I don't want to let the other players in on it, but if I win the tournament, I'll tell you Sunday night."

Ben Hogan, whom the public thought of as grim and humorless, was six strokes behind, but provided the biggest laugh of the week the following morning when he approached Nelson's wife at breakfast, and inquired: "I don't want to appear nosey, Louise, but by any chance did Byron talk in his sleep last night?"

Hogan managed well enough without the secret, however, which seemed to evaporate on the weekend, perhaps carried away by a gust of wind. After falling further behind, he began closing the gap on Nelson over the last two rounds, posting scores of 67 and 70. When Lord Byron bogied the seventeenth hole on Sunday, he needed a birdie at the last to win, a par to survive.

The eighteenth hole at Augusta National bends around a tall pine forest that crowds close along its right flank, and it was here that the dreadful thing happened. Nelson's foot slipped as he swung, causing a high push that sent his ball deep into the forest. Byron could punch his ball out sideways, but that would leave him with a wood or long-iron to the green. As he looked around, he spied an opening above him that led through the branches but to the right of the green.

"You can nearly always escape if you have room to swing, and luckily I did,"Nelson recalled. "But I had to hook it." There he was, feet below the ball, making the hook easier to play, but needing first to steer the ball through the little window high above him. He judged the green to be 180 yards away.

"I hit a five-iron solidly. It sailed through the opening and onto the green as pretty as you please," Nelson smiled, "and I almost made a three." His putt, from close to twenty feet, just grazed the hole. The wonderful thing had happened.

The eighteen-hole playoff the next day was all one could hope to see from these two. Even the pros stayed to watch, something they rarely did. Playing immaculate golf, Hogan led by three strokes after five holes. He played the next eleven holes in one under par, but lost five strokes to Nelson. On and on they went, neither man giving an inch, with the issue in doubt until the last. It was bloodcurdling stuff. Nelson finally won by a single stroke, scoring 69 to Hogan's 70, and earning his second Masters.

There have been memorable playoffs for the Masters, but none quite like this one. Asked to rate the most dramatic finishes of all the Masters through 1960, Bob Jones listed Sarazen's in 1935 as the greatest, and this one just behind it. Curiously, this was only the second time in their professional careers, so parallel in every way, that Nelson and Hogan met in a playoff.

The first was a playoff for the Texas Open in 1940, which Nelson won. The pair did meet in match play twice—the caddie championship at Glen Garden Country Club in 1926, and the quarterfinals of the PGA Championship in 1941—and Nelson won each time. Hogan would go on to surpass Nelson in tour victories, and win the four major championships—something Nelson failed to accomplish—while Nelson retired early after winning everything in sight during those two magical years of his in the mid-1940s.

The pros are unsentimental in assessing the strengths and weaknesses of their rivals. Paul Runyan, the terrier-sized terror of the 1930s when he won two PGA Championships and twice led the tour in earnings, later became one of golf's finest teachers. He was a keen student of the games of the great players, most of whom he had observed at firsthand. People will debate forever, it seems, the relative strengths of Hogan, Nelson, and Snead, as they will any of the great players.

Hogan is generally accorded the nod in these discussions, largely on the strength of his four U.S. Open titles. Yet the question lingers. "Hogan had a psychological disadvantage when facing Nelson," Paul Runyan observed, when asked to compare the two some time ago. "Ben was jealous of him. Nelson didn't have a jealous bone in his body." There it is, bald and honest. Is that, in the end, all that stood between these two?

Jock and Freddie

Two aged figures move slowly across the freshly-cut lawn in front of the Augusta National clubhouse. The warm Georgia sun splashes through the early April morning, releasing the faint, familiar smell of pines and flowers.

A sweatered gallery has already begun to drift away from the putting green toward the starting box where officials in trim green blazers and white slacks wait quietly inside thin yellow ropes for another Masters Tournament to begin.

It is April 1971. One of the two old men is Freddie McLeod. He won the United States Open in 1908. He is the shortest man, at five-foot-four, to win it. He is 88. The other is Jock Hutchison, winner of the 1920 PGA Championship and the 1921 British Open. He is 86. McLeod and Hutchison are the honorary starters at the Masters Tournament, a ritual they have enacted every year since 1963. McLeod competed in the first Masters in 1934. Hutchison's first was the following year, 1935.

They are native Scots, Hutchison of St. Andrews and McLeod of North Berwick, friends of half a century, and two of the last surviving links to the original Scottish invasion of

American golf. They are also the last survivors of the days when all past U.S. Open and PGA champions played here. Now, because the touring pros demanded more spots in the Masters, only Masters champions are forever eligible.

Hutchison and McLeod are led inside the ropes. They pose for photographs. Behind them, their white-uniformed caddies hold aloft signs bearing their contestant's numbers. The numbers are their ages. Hutchison wears brown trousers, a white cap and yellow turtleneck jersey with matching cardigan sweater. McLeod is turned out in a bright orange cardigan over a white button-down shirt with red, white, and blue striped tie, grey cuffed slacks, and a brown fedora. He wears thick eyeglasses.

There is a momentary lull, and Hutchison asks a man in the gallery, "Do you know how much a Scotsman can drink?" He waits craftily. When the man shrugs, Jock cackles, "Any given amount." The crowd smiles. McLeod and Hutchison are wired for sound by two technicians for a film being made about the Masters. One of the technicians demonstrates how the microphone works and fumbles while putting the battery unit in Hutchison's hip pocket. "Well, alright, laddie, but dinna take me dollar," says Jock in a Scottish brogue. Jess Sweetser, an amateur champion of the 1920s, and Keith Mackenzie, secretary of the Royal & Ancient Golf Club, stop briefly to wish them well.

The first hole at Augusta is a par-four that sweeps up a long hill and curls to the right behind deep bunkers. McLeod is first to hit and drives his ball straight down the center about 160 yards. There is applause and he doffs his hat. Hutchison's turn. He addresses the ball, pauses, and then licks his hands. "I'd rather my wife hit this one," says Jock. He hits an acceptable drive which lands on the right side of the fairway, and asks: "Where did it go? I canna see where the ball goes, that's the hardest thing now."

The pair sets off, McLeod walking with short, careful steps. Hutchison walks with a limp caused by arthritis of the right hip.

Someone calls from the gallery: "We hope you make the cut." McLeod looks around vacantly and snorts: "Make the cut? I'm more concerned about making the hill." A small group separates from the crowd and strings out along both sides of the fairway to follow the two old Scots. Some are friends, others only curious. By the third hole, half of them will be trekking back to the clubhouse. On the green, Hutchison misses a short putt and grumbles. McLeod then leaves a putt short. "That's the trouble with you little light fellows—you canna hit it," Jock says.

At the second tee, Hutchison scrapes a tee shot low and straight. It just clears the forward tee. He makes a face. Freddie reassures him. "It's okay, Jock. You can find your ball. That's all you can expect now." After their third shots on this long par-five, McLeod is forty yards ahead of his companion. Hutchison argues with his caddie, who wants him to hit a wood. Finally, he selects a five-wood. The shot disappears into a bunker in front of the green. "I should have taken the damn three-iron," mutters Jock.

When he reaches the bunker, Jock peers at the sand and says he wishes he had a drink. He makes a fine recovery, then realizes that he is himself trapped in the steeply-banked bunker. He crawls up the side toward the flag and painfully claws his way past the protruding lip. After holing out, he looks at his ball and says: "Well, I've still got the same ball."

McLeod chides him for dawdling with the spectators between green and tee. Despite their ages, they play surprisingly fast. Not as briskly, though, as some tournament officials once thought. "We used to play six holes and then cut over to the sixteenth, skipping the rest. No one ever knew why we finished the round so quickly," Freddie confesses. The pair has not played more than nine holes for many years.

Now they are back at the clubhouse, tired but happy with finishing nine holes before an appreciative gallery. Jock rips off the recording gear. McLeod removes his more carefully, and admonishes: "When you see the Masters picture now, all you said will be in there." Says Jock: "They'll put me in jail for what's in there." A photographer wants them to pose for more pictures. "Do you want to take Mac and me together?" Hutchison asks. "You must want it for the funny sheet." When the photographer finishes, McLeod asks: "Don't we get a drink for this?"

They walk into the white plantation clubhouse and up the winding, green-carpeted staircase to a small changing room beside the bar. Both order Scotch and water. A friend comes in to congratulate them on their round. "I thought Freddie was good, but I was lousy," Jock says. "You were," Freddie agrees.

The banter between them begins to perk up as they talk about the old days. "Freddie got all the good-looking women, and those he didn't want he gave over to me," Jock reminisces. Both deplore the elimination of the stymie rule. "Jock, you could'na lay me a stymie no matter how hard you tried," says McLeod. He turns to a reporter and adds, "I just want you to know I'm two years older than him." "And you look ten years older," Hutchison replies. They order another drink.

McLeod lives in retirement at the club he once served as professional, the Columbia Country Club in Chevy Chase, Maryland. "They gave me a nice apartment in the club, plus board and room, and a pension, and it doesn't cost me a dime," Freddie says, then laughs: "And all the drinks I can drink. I play gin and get lots of sleep." Hutchison, also retired, still receives a salary from the Glen View Country Club in Glenview, Illinois, where he became the professional thirty-eight years earlier.

Neither man seems anxious to end the reunion. They met in 1908 at the Myopia Hunt Club in Hamilton, Massachusetts, where McLeod won the Open and a purse of $300. They look around the room in vain for old friends. "Jock is all that's left," says McLeod. "Billy Burke doesn't come any more. Some of my younger friends still come—Gene Sarazen, Julius Boros, and Art Wall. And Arnold Palmer. He says hello. He never called me anything but 'pro.' There is nothing like the Masters anywhere in the world. It seems like everyone here knows golf. For some reason, all the Masters have great finishes. I'll never forget the year Palmer finished 2-3-3 to beat Venturi." His voice trails off.

Hutchison will leave shortly with his wife and relatives and go on to Ft. Lauderdale where he owns a winter home. McLeod will visit with the fifteen or twenty Columbia Country Club members who accompany him each year to the Masters, then spend the afternoon sitting in a solitary white chair on the veranda watching the Masters unfold yet again.

The Ghost of
Billy Joe

⊷⇒ ० ० ० ⇐⊷

In 1954, the Masters was turned on its magnolia blossoms by
an impetuous, appealing amateur named Billy Joe Patton. A
native of Morganton, North Carolina, Patton was not entirely
unknown in amateur golf circles, but he was hardly a household
name. He had secured his invitation to the Masters by less than
heroic means, having been chosen an alternate for the Walker
Cup team the previous summer—a route into the Masters that
no longer exists.

Not a man to take seriously, people thought, nor one to take
himself too seriously, as things turned out. Nevertheless, Patton
would deliver his share of heroics that week.

All he did was share the first round lead with E. J. "Dutch"
Harrison (one of the wiliest and most underrated pros of his
generation), lead the tournament all by himself after two
rounds, and then, after surrendering the lead to Ben Hogan in
the third round, roar back to overtake both Hogan and Snead in
the final round aided by a mighty stroke that found the cup at

the sixth and allowed Billy Joe to post the magic numeral "1" on his card.

Patton was thirty-two, and seemed to play without fear. He had adopted a bold, attacking style as his own even before Palmer made it commonplace. He had a fast swing and a fast quip, and played, then and now, with a minimum of fuss and a maximum of enthusiasm. He had a ripe sense of humor, too. Writing in *Golf Journal* of Patton's nomination in 1982 for the Bobby Jones Award, given by the USGA for sportsmanship, Bob Sommers relates this anecdote, which remains a favorite:

During a close match in Pinehurst's North-South Amateur, which he won three times, incidentally, Patton had pulled his drive onto a mound next to a road. As he contemplated the awkward stance, a woman motorist saw him and stopped, calling to him from her car to inquire where she might find a room in Pinehurst. Billy Joe neither hesitated nor changed his stance, retorting: "In about ten minutes, you can have mine."

By the time Patton reached the bait-and-snare thirteenth on Sunday's final round in 1954, he was tied for the lead with Snead and Hogan. The thirteenth is a short par-five, just 475 yards long, shaped across a wooded hillside that falls to the left toward Rae's Creek which follows the length of the hole and crosses in front of the green. Behind the green are flowering azaleas and magnolia in a setting that is one of the lushest, most colorful in golf.

Everything about this hole invites a player to gamble, which played to Billy Joe's natural tendencies. He cracked a fine drive down the left side of the fairway, well past playing partner Jimmy Demaret, leaving Patton in favorable position to go for the green in two. "There never was a doubt that I should go for the green," he said afterward. "People forget that I had won the driving contest that week with a belt of 338 yards; I had the distance to reach it easily."

There was a puff of wind against him, but the ball was in a

good lie. The only thing he discussed with his caddie was "whether to burn a two-iron in there, or hit an easy four-wood." Patton chose the wood and took dead aim at the flagstick, which was cut into the back right portion of the green. The club made solid contact, but as the ball rose it drifted a few feet off line, hit into the fringe, and bounced onto the apron, then rolled over the bank into the shallow water below.

"It wasn't that bad a golf shot; in fact, it was one of the best I've ever hit, only it drifted right on me," said Patton. The water was shallow enough to allow him to play from the creek, so he removed his shoes and made his way to the ball. But facing a slippery stance in deep rough, he feared he wouldn't get the ball up the steep bank to the green, so he elected to drop. Barefooted now, Patton pitched weakly into the fringe, and his next went six feet past the hole.

"I'd played barefooted half the time I was growing up, so I was used to it. I may have rushed the shot, though, because I noticed the twosome coming up the fairway behind us, but that's tournament golf." He missed the putt coming back, the first of that distance he had missed all week, and finally holed in seven. At about that time, Hogan plunked a ball into the pond beside the eleventh green, an unpardonable sin for this otherwise unflappable thinker, and made a double-bogey of his own.

The mishap at thirteen might have rattled other golfers, but Patton wasn't finished. On the next hole, he hit an eight iron to within inches, and holed in three, to regain one of his lost strokes. Then, trying for extra distance at the fifteenth, he hooked his drive onto a bare lie. "I tried to hit a two-wood to the green and bellied it straight into the pond," Billy Joe recalled. "After dropping, I hit a super pitch to within five feet of the cup, then missed the downhill putt, just like I did at thirteen." With that bogey, Patton dropped a stroke behind Snead and Hogan, and that's how they finished.

Afterward, the press clamored to know why Billy Joe chose to go for the greens at both par-fives? Why take the risk at thirteen while holding a piece of the lead, they asked? He admitted his judgment at fifteen was poor, but not at thirteen. "People said I was crazy to go for it, but they aren't knowledgeable about golf," said Patton. "There was nothing wrong with my strategy. I had played a daring, brave brand of golf all week, which is my natural style, and it had produced half my birdies. Nobody called me reckless when I made the hole-in-one."

Just the opposite of Hogan's methodical approach. Paired with Jackie Burke, Ben played the thirteenth with a controlled drive to the middle of the fairway and a careful pitch short of the creek. Burke knocked his on in two, then watched Ben pitch close with his third and tap in for birdie. Burke asked why he hadn't gone for the green. "I didn't think I needed a three," replied Hogan, with a withering stare.

At the presentation ceremony, Bob Jones handed Patton a gold medal for finishing low amateur, and addressed these words to the gallery: "If anyone ever created a stir in golf, he did. He has no cause for regret, because he finished one stroke behind the two greatest golfers in the world." By this slender margin, Patton had lost his bid to become the first and, to date, the only amateur to win the Masters, an outcome that surely would have warmed Jones's heart.

Billy Joe had neither regrets, nor apologies. "I don't feel bad about those two holes, and I don't want you to feel bad about them, either," he told the gallery at the awards ceremony. "When I left Morganton to play in this tournament, I told myself I'd take a shot at every pin, if I could. I had lots of breaks this week, and I got those sevens and those sixes the same way I got all those birdies."

Patton's ghost has haunted the Masters ever since, and hovers over the thirteenth like an omen. Whenever a player follows Billy Joe into oblivion, as Curtis Strange in 1985 and so many others have done, the ghost is trotted out again. In 1984, Ben

Crenshaw came to this spot in the final round and faced the classic decision to go for the green, or not. He caught a glimpse of Patton standing on the hillside, laid up safely, and went on to win. Afterward, he credited Patton for inspiring him to the right choice. The trouble with Crenshaw's account is that Patton, who has served as a rules official at this hole on many occasions, was nowhere near the place in 1984. The power of suggestion, no doubt.

It has been nearly half a century since Patton's great gamble that failed. It's worth venturing a penny or two that his heroic near-miss and the sporting instincts that gave it life will continue to haunt the place as long as the Augusta National continues to hoist its flag each spring.

Mr. Marr, Mr. Roberts, and Mr. Hogan

✦◦◦◦✦

Dave Marr never won the Masters, but he had an interesting run at Augusta in the decade between 1960 and 1970. He finished in the top forty in his first try, and tied for second, with Nicklaus, behind Arnold Palmer in 1964. Altogether, Marr played in nine Masters, and missed a few cuts, too, but he never forgot that maiden appearance in 1960.

"It was a tremendous experience, more than you could imagine no matter how much people described it to you," said Marr. "To see Bob Jones, to experience the whole atmosphere and the awards presentation, and the wonderful way you were treated was unlike any other tournament I've been to. I was impressed, as everyone was, with how smoothly and completely Clifford Roberts ran things.

"Of course, Mr. Roberts always thought I was Dick Mayer. I guess he thought we looked alike," said Marr. "Whenever he saw me, he asked about my winning the U.S. Open at Inverness in 1957, which, of course, Dick did, while I didn't even qualify for the Open until 1960. I was about half scared of Mr. Roberts, you know, so I never corrected him. 'Yes sir, I beat Middlecoff in that playoff, you bet,' I'd say to him.

"What was I gonna do? Are you gonna tell Mr. Roberts he's wrong? In Augusta? No sir, not me," said Marr. "I'll come back here forever, if I can, and darned if I'll do anything to jeopardize my chances."

As long as you went by the rules, Marr recalled, and didn't make demands for special treatment, such as requesting six extra badges, you were treated with the utmost warmth and courtesy. Marr never did so, but, in his first Masters, he forgot his player's badge one day. He had credentials to enter the grounds, but a player's badge is needed to enter the locker room. This happened to be a tournament day, not a practice day, and Marr was on a schedule leading to his tee time. At the door to the players' locker room stood a Pinkerton guard, with whom Dave had been friendly through the early part of the week.

"Good morning, Dave," said the guard, with a smile.

"Good morning," said Dave, smiling pleasantly.

"Where's your badge?" asked the guard, with a smile.

Marr was wearing a visor that day, and quickly reached up to locate the badge, but it wasn't there.

"I must have left it at the house," said Marr, not smiling quite so broadly.

"You'll need your badge," said the guard, pleasantly but firmly.

Marr looked at the guard steadily: "You know who I am?"

"Yes, I do," replied the guard.

"And I can't come in, is that what you're saying?" Dave inquired.

The guard looked Marr straight in the eye: "If I let you in, Mr. Roberts will fire me."

"That's good enough for me," replied Marr, who turned on his heel, walked to the parking lot, drove home, retrieved his badge, and returned to the Augusta National grounds. Not a peep from Marr.

"This guy wasn't being a little dictator trying to exercise a little power" Marr said later. "He just let me know it would cost him his job if he let me in, and he said it very nicely. It made perfect sense to me, so I just went back and got the badge without complaint. I'll never forget how he handled the situation. That was thirty years ago, and since then lots of tournaments have adopted the practices developed at the Masters, but this is an example of why the Masters was, and still is the best run tournament in the world."

That week, Marr had played a practice round with Ben Hogan. The pair came to the long, uphill eighth where the fairway seems to disappear in the distance and the green vanishes behind a cluster of tall pines on the left. During the tournament, a forecaddie is stationed at the top of the hill to signal players in the fairway below when the green is clear.

By then, Hogan's injuries had begun to take their final toll; his legs were no longer able to carry the violent speed he once generated. Always an immaculate strategist, Hogan liked to hit his second shot on this par-five to the top of the hill, rather than try for the green.

"Whether the forecaddie was there or not, Ben always placed his second up there so he could walk up and rest before hitting his third shot," said Marr, who continued the story by saying he was playing well this day. "I'm in red figures, and Ben's about even par. I got him by the throat, you know, only it's about twenty years too late. I drove into the fairway bunker, and I've got about 280 yards to the green and need to clear a lip that's about five-feet tall. It's a six-iron, tops, to get the ball over that lip.

"While I'm standing there daydreaming, Ben walks over, peers at my ball, and says with that deep, resonant voice of his: 'You think you can get home from here?' The forecaddie had not signaled us on, but I grabbed my six-iron from the bag, jumped in the bunker, and made a wild pass at the ball. Luckily, the shot reached the top of the hill. I had forgotten that Hogan was waiting to go. I mean, the man as much as told me to 'hit it, goddammit, you're away.' You're supposed to wait until the forecaddie waves you on, but Hogan wasn't about to wait for anybody or anything. And I sure wasn't gonna try to correct him. Would you?"

In 1964, the year Marr finished second to Arnold Palmer, he was paired with Hogan in Friday's second round. Marr had played a lot of golf with Hogan at Seminole, where Hogan practiced each spring and where Dave was once an assistant under Claude Harmon.

"I would always greet him each morning as he went by the golf shop," Marr said. "I'd say, 'Good morning, Mr. Hogan,' and he'd nod and continue on his way. One morning, he turned around and came back."

"Dave, don't ever call anybody Mister that you may one day have to play," said Hogan. He turned and went to the practice tee.

"I've never forgotten that," Marr said. "From that morning, it was, 'Good morning, Ben.' Why would he say that to a kid the age of twenty? I have no idea, but there was a side to him that was not apparent to everyone.

"That round together in the Masters was one of the thrills of my life," said Marr, "because the galleries were applauding him everytime we walked onto a green. I finally got to where I was walking twenty yards behind him, the hairs rising on the back of my neck every time he approached another green.

"How do you not touch your cap? How do you not choke? I would have been crying, people welcoming you to each hole like that with a standing ovation," said Marr. "Ben handled it very quietly. In his own way, I think Hogan thought it was terrific, but he wasn't going to let it interfere with his business. It was a scene I'll never forget, and neither, I feel sure, will any of the people who witnessed it."

In one of those extraordinary ironies that life deals to us, Hogan and Marr passed away within months of each other in 1997. A friendship had grown between the two in later years, an unlikely meeting of different generations based on a common interest, a mutual affection, a sense of humor, and the stubborn refusal to give in to the grisly, final scorekeeper that seeks us all.

Dead Man

→══○ ○ ○ ○══←

The caddies who ply their trade at the Augusta National Golf Club were once among the best known in the game. Before the pros were given permission to bring their own in 1983, Augusta's caddies were used exclusively in the Masters and many became celebrities of a sort. There was Gene Sarazen's famous caddie, Stovepipe, and Ironman, who toted for Arnold Palmer. There was Reindeer, a huge man with hands the size of catcher's mitts, who could catch full shots in his prodigious paws, sometimes on the fly, yet had peculiar notions about how certain putts would break on Augusta National's famously mutinous greens.

And then there was Cemetery, a name given to one of the caddies by former President Dwight Eisenhower. Before Eisenhower became a member of the Augusta National Golf Club, Willie Perteet was known as Dead Man. The story was uncovered by Will Grimsley, golf writer for the Associated Press, who found out that Dead Man's nickname had been earned "after he was chopped up in a knife fight and laid out on a morgue slab, apparently for dead." Perteet kept the nickname until Eisenhower joined the club and gave him a new one. "The President told me all dead men belong in cemeteries," said Willie, "so from now on he'd call me Cemetery."

He became Ike's favorite caddie, and the President was Willie's favorite loop. Like any reasonable fellow, Eisenhower would show his temper on occasions. "He get the red neck sometimes," said the caddie of the President, "and get his dander up when he miss a shot, but I shore love to caddie for that man." The temper dwindled after Ike's heart attacks. "He don't get as het up as before the attacks, but he still work himself up into a lather over that golf game," said Cemetery. "He be hitting the ball farther—235 yards sometimes—but he cain't get a putt to fall for love or mercy. And that 10-iron of his—his bettin' iron—well, that's been misbehavin' too."

Then, in 1957, Willie was fired as Eisenhower's caddie, and the story hit the newspapers. Cemetery had become a famous caddie, and of course Eisenhower was the nation's most famous golfer. But head pro Ed Dudley had decided Cemetery, now fifty-one, was getting too slow to keep up with the President, who was Dudley's regular playing partner at the Augusta National. "The President plays like a whirlwind," said Dudley. "He hits the ball and, whoosh, he's gone. It takes a young man to keep up with him, so I had to make a change."

"I don't know what I done wrong," said Cemetery. "I guess Mr. Dudley thought I was gettin' old, but I don't like this talk that I'm decrepit and ready for the rockin' chair. I ain't ready for the grave yet, and don't be remindin' me 'bout my name bein' Cemetery. Mr. Dudley know what he's doin' and I sure don't plan to make a fuss, but if he think I slowed up, he shoulda seen me at the night club last night and early this mornin'."

Cemetery had caddied since childhood. Dudley made it clear that he would not lose his place on the caddie staff of the Augusta National: "We just thought it advisable to give the President a younger, more alert man." Meanwhile, Dead Man was dead, presidentially speaking, though diplomatic: "I hope I don't get in Mister Ike's doghouse on account of this publicity," he said, while slyly enjoying the attention. The other caddies goaded him about his new celebrity. "We heard about you on the radio; you're famous," they said. "I must have missed that," said Cemetery, brightening. "Enlighten me."

The Meanest Little Hole
in the World

The twelfth hole at the Augusta National Golf Club has been called the most demanding par-three in golf by no less an authority than Jack Nicklaus. Many concur. Lloyd Mangrum called it, "the meanest little par-three in the world." More souls have been lost there than went down with the Titanic. Players become so absorbed in the problems at this hole they sometimes lose their sense of time and place. Some ignore their partners, as Ben Hogan did in 1947.

Paired with his chum, Claude Harmon, Hogan carefully judged the conditions at the twelfth tee, then hit one of those majestic iron shots for which he was so famous. The ball landed fourteen feet from the flagstick, a brilliant stroke. However, Harmon struck an even better one; his ball covered the flag and bounced into the hole for an ace. Harmon walked to the green and, with the crowd still cheering, picked his ball from the cup. Hogan then holed a difficult breaking putt for birdie.

As the pair moved up the slight incline to the thirteenth tee,

Hogan was muttering to himself. Reaching the tee first, he surprised Harmon by teeing his ball and preparing to drive first. Shaking his head, Hogan said, "You know, Claude, that's the first time I've ever birdied that hole." Stunned, Harmon sputtered: "But Ben, I have the honor. I made a one!" Hogan stared at him blankly. Remember, Hogan and Harmon were friends.

The twelfth hole will do that to you. So simple a hole, really; by today's standards, a mere flick of 155 yards, and even by yesterday's, no more than a seven-iron without wind. Ah, the wind. There you have it. It is the wind, combined with the clever use of Rae's Creek, that makes this hole the greatest par-three in existence. An overstatement? Perhaps, and perhaps not. As millions have seen on television, the green is placed on a bank above the creek within a grove of trees that separates Augusta National from its older neighbor, the Augusta Country Club.

Old Masters hands remember the extraordinary adventure of Bob Rosburg during one of his first visits to the twelfth hole. The swirling winds that are such a prominent feature of this corner of the golf course were blowing strongly that day, and Rosburg was undecided about his club selection. He was paired with Moe Norman, the unorthodox but gifted Canadian whose reputation for ball striking was near-legendary.

It was a blustery day, and Norman had gone for the middle of the wide, shallow green with a five iron. His ball made it halfway across Rae's Creek before the winds knocked it down into the water. Rossie debated, and finally chose a four-iron. He made solid contact, but the winds changed direction and his ball rode a sudden gust over the green, over the bunkers and the hill behind it onto the grounds of the Augusta Country Club.

Rosburg put down another ball, and, with the very same club, stroked this one to within five feet of the cup and made four, for the prettiest cross-country, two-course bogey anyone is likely to see. Rosburg, of course, went on to become a television commentator, and, after a patchy start, one of its best. "It seems to me now that the wind doesn't blow there as much as it used to," said Rosburg. "Maybe it's because the trees have grown so much taller, but the wind used to just kill you at this hole, and holes like the third and fourth which are built on the high side of the golf course."

And then there is the extraordinary adventure of Tom Weiskopf at this maddening hole. It is not fair to repeat his sad story every April nor to dwell on the misfortunes of a fellow human being. It's just not fair to keep referring to that horrible incident, but life is not fair, and neither is golf. Tom did not always accept this during his days as a player, but the notion seems to have grown on him since becoming a golf architect.

Tom was struggling through the first round in the 1980 Masters when he reached the twelfth hole. Weiskopf had been a perennial favorite because his power game seemed to suit the golf course, and four times in the previous decade had finished second in the tournament, which tied a record established by Ben Hogan. But, now, he found water with his tee shot, and, after dropping short of the creek, dunked another. Stunned, the gallery and millions more on television watched Tom hit three more into Rae's Creek before reaching the green and finally holing out in thirteen strokes.

What possessed the man? After Weiskopf's appalling thirteen, one of the pros watching in the locker room quipped that Tom had "shot his age." The pros can be merciless with one another. Unfortunately, that wasn't the end of it. The next day, Weiskopf reached the scene of the massacre and plunked two more into Rae's Creek. He wrote down a seven, which gave him a total of twenty strokes for his two tries at the little twelfth, a fast fourteen over par. In twelve years, Tom had never before gone in the water at this hole.

Weiskopf's score is a record. Previous to this, the mark was held by Dow Finsterwald, who made an eleven after hitting four balls into the water in 1951, a record he was happy to see eclipsed. What about his good pal, Arnold Palmer? In 1959, Arnie was defending his title and leading the tournament when he came to the twelfth. His tee shot dropped into the creek, his next went over the green, and he finally holed in six. The triple bogey cost him dearly; Palmer finished just two strokes behind the winner, Art Wall.

In one Masters, Gary Player putted off the twelfth green—twice, on consecutive days. During the first Masters, when the nines were reversed, this little hole was the third. Errie Ball had a birdie try from six feet, and knocked the putt into a bunker. Ball, the great-nephew of England's amateur legend, John Ball, was then an assistant at East Lake Country Club in Atlanta, Bob Jones's home club, and a terrific young player. "That hole was always intimidating, even then. It gave us the shakes," said Ball.

Sam Snead once made an eight here, and withdrew. Another time, Toney Penna hit the flagstick with his tee shot, then made five. Gene Sarazen, leading the first round of a postwar Masters, knocked three straight into the water and picked up. In 1985, Payne Stewart hit a solid eight-iron into the back bunker. His next rolled across the green into the water, and his subsequent pitch into the green spun back into the same water. This was followed by yet another pitch into the back bunker, from which point he took four to get down. A nine, which swiftly removed him from contention.

No one is immune from the mental pressures on this hole. Consider the performance of the greatest Masters winner of them all, Jack Nicklaus. A double-bogey at twelve cost him the Masters in 1981, when he finished two strokes behind Tom Watson, and, in 1991, he made a seven on this hole, the first quadruple-bogey he had ever posted in the Masters. In 1964, as defending champion, Jack apparently thought too much about this shot, and shanked it. He finished second to Palmer that year, then won the next two Masters. Thirty-one years later, in the second round, Jack repeated his pitch-out at the same hole; after studying the winds swirling above the creek, he hit another of the dreaded unmentionables.

Two shanks and a quad at the same hole for the greatest player in history? That should be evidence enough for any jury. Mangrum had it right—the meanest little hole in golf.

Amateur Wizards

When Bob Jones issued the first invitations for his new Augusta National Invitational, to be played in March 1934, two dozen went to fellow amateurs. Fourteen, including Jones himself, accepted and actually played. In Jones's vision, amateurs were to be an integral part of the fabric of the tournament, as they are of the game, a tradition that happily survives.

In recent years, until Matt Kuchar's splash in 1998, amateurs have not fared too well, but several times in the past amateurs have contended and nearly won. Two, in fact, are members of the Augusta National: Billy Joe Patton and Charlie Coe. Another member, Charlie Yates, played in a dozen Masters and was low amateur several times. Yates, a friend of Bob Jones and a fellow Atlantan, also won the British Amateur in 1938, and after laying down his competitive cudgels took on the duties of running the press operations at the Masters.

During an extraordinary streak of fifteen years, from 1947 to 1961, five different amateurs made serious bids for Masters titles. In 1947, Frank Stranahan fired 68 in the final round to tie Byron Nelson for runner-up honors, two strokes behind the winner, Jimmy Demaret, and one stroke in front of Ben Hogan. Pretty tall company, that. Stranahan was a wealthy playboy who was determined to show he was the equal of the pros, and had worked tirelessly on his game and his physique.

If not quite a peer of Nelson, Snead, and Demaret, he had nevertheless won a tour event in Durham sixteen months earlier as a twenty-three-year-old amateur, and would go on to finish joint runner-up in the British Open in both 1947 and 1953, and win the British Amateur championship twice, in 1948 and 1950. Frank Stranahan was never again a threat in the Masters, but with that fine performance in 1947, he became the first amateur to finish so high.

In 1954, Sam Snead won his third green jacket, but not before surviving a playoff with his great rival, Ben Hogan, nor dodging a terrific challenge from the brash amateur, Billy Joe Patton. Patton, 32, was in the field as an alternate, not even a full member of the Walker Cup team. Nevertheless, this genial North Carolinian shared the first round lead with Dutch Harrison, then found himself in the lead all by himself after two rounds, one stroke ahead of Ben Hogan. Patton fell behind in the third round, but took the lead once again on Sunday.

Still leading at the thirteenth, Billy Joe gambled with his long second; his ball bounded into the creek, which cost him double bogey. Toying with destiny and smiling as he did, Patton later bogeyed the fifteenth, again gambling, yet still he finished with a 71, only one stroke behind Hogan and Snead. Had he gone for par at either hole, how different things might have been. Patton settled for the low amateur medal, an honor he would capture twice more.

In 1956, the two hottest amateurs in American golf were Ken Venturi and Harvie Ward. Harvie was the reigning U. S. Amateur champion, and would win the title again later that summer, but Ken Venturi was twenty-four, hungry, and fearless. He was on a high because he had just beaten Ward in the San Francisco

City Championship, and prior to the Bing Crosby tournament at Pebble Beach the two "lads" had played a famous challenge match at Cypress Point against Byron Nelson and Ben Hogan— amateurs vs. the pros—in which the pros barely scratched out a win on the last hole.

In the Masters that spring, Venturi blistered the course in 66 the first day, followed that with 69, and led the Masters at the halfway point. He faltered in the third round, but so did everyone else. With one round to go, he led by four strokes. His closest pursuer, Cary Middlecoff, limped in with 77 that final day, but Venturi staggered to an 80, a devastating finish. His loss, by one stroke, came at the hands of Jack Burke, Jr., who started the final round eight shots behind the leader. Burke holed a long putt at seventeen for birdie, and closed with 71 while posting the biggest fourth round turnaround in Masters history.

In 1957, it was Harvie Ward's turn to threaten the pros. Ward had tied for eighth in the 1955 Masters, and in 1957 was playing "the best golf of my career." His long game was solid, and Ward was one of the great putters in the game. Ever. With two U.S. Amateur crowns and a British Amateur title under his belt, Harvie was confident and cool under pressure, unruffled by the big names. In practice rounds with Byron Nelson, Ward shot two 69s and played so brilliantly that Nelson picked the young amateur to win.

"For a long time I sorta felt that the amateurs just filled out the field in the Masters," said Harvie. "Then Billy Joe in 1954 and Kenny in 1956 almost won, and I began to realize maybe an amateur could win this thing."

Reaching the sixteenth hole in the third round, Ward realized he was only a stroke from the lead, and a birdie at one of the remaining holes would tie him for the lead. Paired with defending champion Jack Burke, Ward lofted a four-iron to within three feet of the cup, then missed the putt. Burke stared in disbelief. At seventeen, Harvie's five-footer spun out; another birdie chance gone.

At the eighteenth, with the flag in front, Ward was short with his second and chipped from the apron; the ball struck the flagstick, and hung on the lip. A 71 that might have been a 68, and still a stroke behind the leader, Sam Snead. Despite the misses, Harvie had eight one-putt greens on the day using a wooden-shafted blade putter he had owned for a dozen years. Fate, however, had decided that both Snead and Ward would lose the next day to Doug Ford's sensational closing round of 66, which was highlighted by a hole-out on his last shot from a fried-egg lie in the greenside bunker at the eighteenth. Harvie finished fourth, behind Ford, Snead, and Jimmy Demaret.

The best pure amateur to have played in the Masters, after Bobby Jones himself, may have been Charlie Coe. His rivals all knew it, too. "Charlie Coe was the best of us, the only guy I really feared out there," said his longtime amateur rival, Harvie Ward. When Coe won the U.S. Amateur in 1949 at Oak Hill, he met Ward in the quarterfinals. Said Harvie: "I had him three down with five to go, and he beat me on the nineteenth hole. He could play with anyone."

The slender Oklahoman would win another U.S. Amateur title in 1958, and nearly won the Masters in 1961, at age thirty-eight, when he finished in a tie with Arnold Palmer, one stroke behind the winner, Gary Player. Over the final two rounds, Coe gained five strokes on Player and four on Palmer with a pair of 69s. On Sunday, paired with Palmer, Coe had a makeable putt for eagle on the par-five fifteenth, and another for birdie at the eighteenth—one that might have brought victory, and the other that would have sent him into a playoff. Charlie Coe finished in the top ten three times, and six times he was low amateur in the Masters in a span that covered twenty-two years from 1949 to 1970, a tournament amateur record likely to stand.

Prior to Frank Stranahan's tie for second in 1947, the best amateur finishes were Lawson Little's sixth place in 1935 and Johnny Dawson's ninth place in 1936. In addition to those already mentioned, others who fared well were Tommy Tailer in 1938, Charles Yates in 1939 (tied with Chick Harbert), and Yates again in 1940, Dick Chapman in 1941, Cary Middlecoff in 1946, Skee Riegel in 1948, Johnny Dawson again in 1949 (tied with Coe), Chuck Kocsis in 1952, Jack Nicklaus in 1960 (tied with Patton), Ben Crenshaw in 1972, Curtis Strange in 1976, and Lindy Miller in 1978. All finished in the top twenty, and won low amateur honors. Matt Kuchar in 1998 missed the top twenty by one stroke, but earned the low amateur medal and a return invitation.

The best year for amateurs was 1954, when five finished in the top twenty—Billy Joe Patton, third; Dick Chapman, eleventh; Ken Venturi, tied for sixteenth; and the pair of Harvie Ward and Charlie Coe, tied for twentieth.

And, finally, what of Bob Jones's own performance? In 1934, he finished at 294, tied for thirteenth place with Walter Hagen and Denny Shute, three strokes better than the next amateur, his friend and fellow Augusta National member, Charles Yates. Over a technicality in the Rules of Golf, the United States Golf Association had questioned Jones's amateur status because he had received compensation from Spalding for a line of clubs that bore his name, and had appeared in a series of instructional films for Warner Brothers after his retirement in 1930.

A mild controversy arose in the press, wanting to know if Jones should be identified as amateur or not. This was solved when Jones, with a nudge from Cliff Roberts, decided that participants in the tournament would be designated neither professional nor amateur, but simply by name. This practical solution, this gesture of deference and courtesy was typical of a man who had lived by the rules all his life.

But, can there have been a doubt in anyone's mind, then or now, that Bobby Jones was always an amateur in his mind and spirit, and in the hearts of golfing fans around the world?

Mackenzie's Request

✦⇥◗ ○ ○ ○ ◖⇤✦

Anyone who has read his book, *The Spirit of St. Andrews*, will know of Alister Mackenzie's prickly nature and anyone who had dealings with Clifford Roberts, Augusta National's first chairman, will know of his stony truculence. Though Mackenzie was a medical doctor long before he became a golf architect, not much evidence of his bedside manner has come down to us. What is apparent from his books and letters, however, is that the warm Scottish blood he inherited from his father sometimes ran close to the surface, nor did he bother to hide that quick, deep temper of his when he wished to express himself forcefully.

After roaming the Fruitlands Nurseries property with Bob Jones in 1931 and planning the holes for the Augusta National course, Mackenzie went to Scotland to work out the design, then returned to New York to present the plans to Clifford Roberts and the construction firm, Olmsted Brothers. Mackenzie oversaw the shaping of the holes in Augusta during the summer of 1932, then departed for California where he had taken up residence in Santa Cruz to work on his course at Pasatiempo.

Soon, he began feeling the pinch of the Depression, as most everyone was, and wrote to Roberts asking for partial payment of his design fee.

In the letter, Mackenzie mentioned that his cash flow had slowed to a trickle, that he was down to his last one hundred dollars, and had even been obliged to sell his golf clubs. Roberts replied politely but firmly in the negative, stating that the club was not in a position to advance funds at this time, adding sternly that Mackenzie should consider himself "lucky to have the $100."

Some time later, Roberts contacted Mackenzie at his home, which bordered the sixth fairway at Pasatiempo, notifying him that his presence was required immediately in Augusta to over-see modifications to certain holes. In his Scottish brogue, which could be made thicker to suit the occasion, Mackenzie gruffly declined, but offered to send one of his "design associ-ates" instead. The design associate he chose was Marion Hollins, one of the most prominent sportswomen of the day, a fine golfer, and the driving force behind the creation of both Cypress Point and Pasatiempo. But she was a woman, after all, and the Augusta National was a men's club. We don't know whether or not Hollins made it to Augusta, although there is photographic evidence that she played an exhibition with Bobby Jones in Atlanta at about that time, but Mackenzie had made his point.

So would Cliff Roberts. Alister Mackenzie never returned to Augusta, and the great man died in January 1934, just months before the first Masters was to be played. In 1935, the Augusta National went into technical bankruptcy, and was reconstituted as a corporation rather than a partnership, its original form. Mackenzie's design fee of $5,600 may have been a casualty of the transaction. The point has not been entirely resolved, al-though the letters exchanged between Roberts and Mackenzie are among the archives stored in the upstairs library of the Augusta National clubhouse.

In the clash of wills between Roberts and Mackenzie, the sharpest word may have been Alister Mackenzie's, but the last, as usual, was Cliff Roberts's.

Snead Resplendent

✦══ ∘ ∘ ∘ ══✦

Sam Snead's immense power and soft touch in the little shots made him a huge gallery favorite and a perennial betting choice to win the Masters ever since his first appearance in 1937, but he had to wait until 1949 to claim his first green jacket. Sam almost won in 1939, his second full year in the big time when he set the tournament record of 280, only to have it snatched away at the end by Ralph Guldahl.

"Slammin' Sammy" Snead was already a star in 1942 when he arrived at the Masters, although he had lost two U.S. Opens he should have won. By then, he had twenty tournament scalps on his belt, including three Canadian Open titles, and would win his first major, the PGA Championship, later that summer. His manager, Fred Corcoran, was a master at generating publicity for his clients. Early that week, he had bragged about Snead's ability to play without shoes. Goaded by Corcoran, Snead removed his shoes in a practice round and played two holes barefooted. He birdied one, and his birdie putt at nine lipped out.

This endeared him to the gallery and press, but Gene Sarazen openly criticized Snead for the stunt, believing the Masters too refined and dignified for such shenanigans and probably defending the image of his good friend, Bob Jones. Snead was a relative youngster compared to Sarazen, the man who had won the most dramatic Masters ever, and who still remained a threat to win. Sarazen's verbal attack only fueled the news stories, which pleased Corcoran.

None of this put a dent in Snead's armor, the toughest in the game. Besides, Sam paid scant attention to things like image and refinement; dignity was for foolish men. Such things were a distraction to the main business of life: winning golf tournaments, fishing and hunting, and collecting female trophies. Snead was good at all of these.

This was the man with the most glorious golf swing in history who thought so little of his dignity that he willingly adopted the croquet style of putting later in his career. Jones despised it, and let Sam know of his disapproval. In fact, Jones is rumored to have encouraged the USGA to ban croquet-style putting, but this only led Snead and others to the side-saddle method, which he soon mastered. There was talk of banning these awkward-looking styles altogether from the Masters, but Jones's sensibilities were ignored, not for the first time. Snead had but one interest in adopting the crouched, ungainly posture this technique required—getting the ball into the hole by whatever means necessary.

Snead's first Masters win came in 1949. His opening rounds of 73-75 were better than they might appear, due to unusually high winds that buffeted the course the first two days. Snead blazed through the last two rounds with matching 67s to clinch the title, a comeback Bob Jones described as "brilliant." In 1952, Snead won again. He and Hogan shared the lead after three rounds. The final round was played in the strongest winds in Masters history. Snead shot 72 to Hogan's 79, and collected his second Masters title. Hogan won it in 1953, the first of his great triple of major championships that year, and the two would meet again in a playoff for the 1954 Masters.

So here were the two champions of golf in 1954, one with the grandest swing in the game who cared little for style or convention, the other with perhaps the most sophisticated and admired technique in history to whom appearance was almost as important as results. Paul Runyan, a contemporary of Snead and Hogan and a shrewd swing analyst, once compared the two. "In match play, Snead was Hogan's equal," said Runyan. "Sam possessed a technical excellence far and away above anyone else of his time. Technically, Sam was better than Ben, but Ben was a better thinker. Snead, though, was a tiger in head-to-head competition."

Not much to choose between them, though. Neither man willing to give an inch, yet each with a healthy respect for the other. Snead had not yet gone to the croquet-style and was still putting well. He was not rolling them in as boldly nor as frequently as in days gone by, but neither was he yipping the short ones. Hogan, however, was beginning to see the decline of his putting skill which, for a decade at least, had been the envy of his peers. Not a few declared emphatically: "Hogan is the best putter in golf from ten feet in."

Hogan always seemed to bring out the best in Snead. "I always enjoyed going head-to-head with Ben," said Sam. "I felt my game rise up a notch when I played him." Hogan would say later, "I've left my blood in every cup of that golf course." He might have been thinking about this playoff, and the one with Nelson in 1942, both of which he lost. Before they teed off, Snead asked Hogan if he wanted to split the purse, something the pros occasionally did in those days. Ben took two drags on his cigarette and said: "Let's play."

"Hogan was awfully long off the tee, almost up with me, but that week he was hitting it crooked, at least by Ben's standards," said Snead. "His short game kept him in the match." Both men turned in 35, and there, at the tenth, Snead holed a murderous downhill chip of sixty-five feet from behind the green to forge into the lead. Hogan evened things at the short twelfth with a par as Snead struggled to make bogey. Snead birdied thirteen to climb back into the lead and gained another stroke at the sixteenth, after laying his approach putt from twenty feet a foot from the cup. Hogan putted weakly from eighteen feet, then missed the next. As Sam was about to tap in the little one that was left, a fan yelled: "Miss it!" but Snead made it.

On eighteen, Hogan drove into a fairway bunker while Snead hit a perfect drive to the right center of the fairway, but in a mushy lie made damp by a sprinkler. Not enough to obtain relief, though. Hogan's shot from the bunker reached the front of the green. "I didn't think he could two-putt from there because the pin was on the back shelf," said Snead. "I played for bogey and hit a safe second into the bunker." Hogan gathered himself, and got down in two putts, but Snead's bogey won the match, 70 to 71, which is about all that separated these two in their careers and in the minds of the fans who saw them play.

Snead, who legend says is the only man in history to have made a hole-in-one with every club in the bag, contended in the Masters into the middle of the next decade. In 1957, Sam finished second to Doug Ford, and in 1958, Snead and Palmer led the tournament after three rounds at five-under par, with Middlecoff a stroke behind. Arnie shot 73 the final day, which normally wouldn't have scared anyone except that Sam shot a closing round of 79, and Middlecoff 75, allowing Palmer to grab his first Masters title. In 1963, Snead tied for third, two strokes behind Nicklaus, who also won his first green jacket on that occasion. Yet another decade passed and, in 1974, Sam was still beating old man par over four rounds, at the age of sixty-two.

His powerful yet graceful swing left an indelible impression on six generations of golfers, and his competitive spirit drove him to become the greatest, most durable winner the game has known. Even his rivals proclaimed Snead one of the glories of the age. It is entirely conceivable, given declining attention spans, that memories of this wonderful player might fade and be lost to future golfers. What an irony that would be. Generations keep searching for the perfect golf swing, and it's been with us all along.

Scorecard Goofs

-»══◦ ◦ ◦ ◦ ══«-

The most vivid memory one has of the 1968 Masters is that of Roberto de Vicenzo trudging from the officials' tent, numb and in despair, after being told of his scorekeeping error in signing a card showing a four on the seventeenth hole instead of the three he actually made. Although the incorrect digit had been marked down by his playing partner and official scorekeeper, Tommy Aaron, Roberto was responsible for checking it. That single mistake cost him the opportunity to meet Bob Goalby in a playoff the next day. Instead, Goalby won the Masters, and de Vicenzo placed second. To his eternal credit, the gallant Roberto blamed only himself and pointed to Goalby's brave performance.

This has been, so far, the most famous scoreboard misstroke in the history of the Masters, but it is not the only one. The first we can find record of occurred in 1953 when Sam Snead was the defender. He had soared to a four-stroke victory over Jack Burke, Jr. in the previous year's Masters, which was marked by heavy weather the last two rounds. Now paired with Byron Nelson in the first round of the 1953 Masters, Snead holed a monster putt of sixty feet on the pitching, final green for a sensational birdie and a round of 70. A nice start, that, but Nelson, who was keeping Sam's card, wrote down a four instead of the three he actually made. Unhappily, Snead signed the card without noticing the mistaken score at the eighteenth hole, and was saddled with an official round of 71. His 70 would have tied him with Hogan, who eventually would win that Masters and go on to capture two other majors that summer, completing one of the greatest single-season performances in history.

Another misstroke occurred in 1957 when the fine amateur, Charlie Coe, handed in an incorrect scorecard at the conclusion of his first round. At first, the committee assessed him a two-stroke penalty, which would have allowed Coe to continue, but changed the decision when reminded that the USGA only recently had issued a ruling mandating disqualification for such infractions. Coe had inadvertently signed for a score lower than the one he made, and it is to his credit that he pointed out the error himself.

In 1960, amateur Dick Chapman was also disqualified for signing an incorrect scorecard. Chapman, the 1940 U.S. Amateur Champion, apparently had knocked his tee shot on the par-three fourth into the bamboo thicket located on the right edge of the hole. Assuming his ball was out of bounds, he played a provisional with appropriate penalty, but later it was determined that the original ball was in bounds and should have been played. The 79 he signed for should have been an 81, after adding two shots for playing the wrong ball, and Chapman was disqualified.

In 1961, the sixth of seven great Turnesa brothers, Jim Turnesa, bogeyed his scorecard when he made a four at the seventh hole, but signed for a five and missed the cut by one stroke. Turnesa, the 1952 PGA champion, had opened with a score of 80, but roared back the second day with a beautifully-shaped round in which he played 69 strokes. That score would have allowed him to make the cut had it not been for the mistaken "5" at the seventh, which turned the 69 into 70, and a ticket out of town.

Neither Turnesa nor Snead lost a tournament as a result of the pencil errors, as de Vicenzo had done, but after Roberto's sad mishap—witnessed by millions on television and criticized for weeks afterward in the media—the Masters officials made changes in the location and arrangements of the scoring table which allowed players to check with scores in greater privacy.

Jones Snaps Back

◦ ◦ ◦

Not long ago, Byron Nelson was reminiscing about the early days of the Masters with Peter Kessler, the smooth, urbane host of an interview show on The Golf Channel. After a round, the players would gather in the clubhouse for drinks, cards, and the usual banter. According to Byron, Bob Jones overheard some of the pros complaining about the "unfair" narrow left side of the third green. The complaints went on for several minutes, perhaps meant for Jones's ears, because he was sitting nearby. Nelson remembers what happened next.

"You guys make me sick," Jones snapped at them. "You think it's your right to birdie every hole. Well, there's such a thing as par, you know, and, on the third hole, the cup is put over on the left side to remind you of it. When the pin is over there, if you'll hit your approach to the right side of the green with a little draw, the ball will run down toward the hole and you'll have a chance to make a birdie."

That's how the hole was designed, Jones implied, reminding them and us that the man revered as the game's greatest gentleman also had a temper. We can all take heart from this, just as we can from his manner of conquering the impulses within and for his well-earned reputation as a sportsman. Gene Sarazen first encountered Jones in 1920 at the U.S. Open held at Inverness in Toledo, Ohio. They were born in 1902, a few weeks apart, and both married women named Mary, one week apart, and both were club throwers.

The two became lifelong friends, an unlikely pairing unless you understood Jones's admiration for the competitive sand he saw in Sarazen, and Sarazen's recognition that, in Jones, he had met a kindred spirit despite the wide gulf in their social backgrounds. Both were bright bulbs, one with a rich educational background, the other without, yet they shared similar beliefs about conduct and decorum, as well as their strong combative impulses.

They frequently played practice rounds together. Neither knew whose club might be launched the farthest, nor earliest, but both realized that the violent behavior had no place on a golf course. They settled on a bet; the first man to throw his club would collect ten dollars from the other. That was quite a lot in those days.

Things went along without incident for several months. Then, one day when the two were paired, Jones hit a clunker. Sarazen turned to his caddie, and said with a crooked smile: "There goes his club, and here comes my ten bucks." But, Jones restrained himself. "I never collected, and I never saw him throw a club again," said Sarazen. Bobby did, though, as he admitted later, but never in public. "Once in a while, I'd let one fly and I got a great deal of relief from it, too, if you want the truth," Jones said.

As we have seen, though, Jones's temper could flare like any man's, particularly if his golf course were criticized by good players whom he felt should know better. He was very clear, for example, about "maintaining greens at such firmness that they will not hold a misplayed shot." Hence, his admonition about the third hole, which, for the very shape of its green, is one of the toughest little par-fours in golf. Complaints are registered about the ninth and fifteenth greens, as well; of late, the players seem to feel the fifteenth has become too punitive because so many of their balls "suck back" off the putting surface into the pond in front.

But that's just the point Jones wanted to make about golf. Not every approach shot must be played by spinning the ball, nor are those types of shots always good golf shots. He would describe them as "misplayed" because they wouldn't hold a green like the fifteenth. As Jones himself said on several occasions, the fifteenth green was designed to be wide and shallow, with a crown, for a purpose. No amount of complaining or caterwauling will change that, although there is a good deal of pressure to do so, even now.

Jones controlled his fury most of the time, but was not above venting his irritation, as any player might. In the first Masters, the great Bobby's putting was described in print as "deplorable" by his good friend, O.B. Keeler. Another scribe wrote of his performance in the first round: "If Runyan had been putting for Jones, he would have been under par. Instead of calling his putter Calamity Jane, call it Bobby's Calamity." That probably stung. After posting 76, Jones strode from the final green, and blurted: "My God, what a round!" He went straight to Clifford Roberts, who was fending off complaints from other players. "Why did you place the pins in such funny places?" he asked the chairman. Roberts explained his reasons, and, after a cool drink of ale, Jones said: "Well, I forgive you, but please don't do it again."

In the second round, Jones knocked his second shot over the green at the thirteenth hole (then played as the fourth). Walking down the fairway with Paul Gallico, one of America's top sportswriters, Jones turned and said: "You know, a man is just as dumb to go over this green as to be short. I got home with a spoon the first day and had a putt for an eagle, but today I just couldn't keep my hand off the brassie, and you know the result." He was irritated with himself.

Then, at the difficult fifth green (now the fourteenth), Jones flubbed his short approach. A mean-hearted spectator applauded, with a sarcastic: "Great shot, Bobby." Jones gave no sign that he had been disturbed by the remark, but as he walked to the next tee, he turned to Keeler and said: "I could shoot him, the way I feel now." The exchange was overheard by Bill Wallace, of the Miami newspaper, who probably sanitized the outburst when he quoted Jones as saying: "I just didn't appreciate the ribbing that fellow gave me. Any other time, I probably would have tried to kill him if I could have gotten near him."

No one has ever said an unkind word about Jimmy Demaret, no one except Bob Jones. Demaret's sunny disposition and fast quips were part of his nature and part of golf lore; even when the barbs stuck, everyone knew Jimmy's intentions were good-humored. In a conversation with a reporter in his hometown of Houston in 1967, Jimmy mentioned that "something was missing from the Masters that year," because the club had begun to limit ticket sales in order to keep the crowds manageable. The story made its way into print.

Jones was livid, and wrote to Demaret, in part: "Over the years, I have seen many television shows in which you have appeared, obviously for monetary remuneration. In not one have I heard you identified as other than 'three times Masters champion.' This would seem to indicate that your position of authority is related very closely to your performance at Augusta, since none of your sponsors has found your other accomplishments so worthy of mention. It is difficult for me to understand how you can continue to depreciate the value of a tournament upon which so much of your prestige rests." Demaret was devastated by Jones's tirade, and couldn't bring himself to attend the Masters for the next six years. He eventually returned in 1974, a little more than two years after Jones's death.

Because of his courteous manners, his intelligence, and his sense of fair play, Jones was idealized even in his twenties as a kind of mythic figure with gentle manners and old-fashioned notions of chivalry. Jones was surely a gentleman and a sportsman, but hardly a society fop. He smoked cigars for pleasure, and cigarettes habitually. He kept a bottle of corn liquor in his locker, and regularly took a nip before a round of golf. He enjoyed off-color stories, and the company of his friends. He loved the outdoors, and spent much of his free time hunting, fishing, and playing tennis. His intellect embraced the law, grand opera, philosophy, mathematics, and politics. As we've seen, he had a temper, and, although he had learned to control it, was not bashful about using it when called upon.

In a letter to Clifford Roberts in 1967, Jones criticized the inflated purses and salaries in professional sports. "The trouble is, we are living in an idiotic society; frankly, if I knew a way to take advantage of the idiots, I would exploit them." A copy of the letter was sent to former President Eisenhower, a member of the Augusta National, who good-naturedly rebuked the author. Jones sent a contrite response: "In my playing days, after making a sour shot, I always got some satisfaction from throwing the club as if it had something to do with the misplay. I finally learned that this should not be done in public, but I still allowed myself this indulgence when playing privately with good friends. Let us just say that, in this case, I allowed myself the luxury of heaving another club." His other considerable merits aside, who could not feel affection for such a man?

Riding High

Oscar Bane Keeler, known simply as O.B., was Bobby Jones's biographer and, because of it, one of the most widely known newspapermen in America. His biography of Jones, *Down the Fairway*, was one of the best-selling golf books of all time. O.B. Keeler, a sportswriter and special correspondent of the *Atlanta Journal*, was a frequent and welcome guest at the Augusta National, as befit the great man's Boswell. Like many of his golfwriting brethren, Keeler had a propensity for drink and, though a gifted writer, was sometimes clumsy.

One night, descending from the second-floor locker room, he slipped on the steep, winding stairs and was headed for a nasty fall. Fortunately, three members were coming up the narrow staircase and broke his fall. This led the members to impose mock sanctions against Keeler, which they did by presenting him with a wheelbarrow for use as a conveyance. In due course, this was captured in a photograph by Frank Christian, Sr., the club's first official photographer.

Years later, when shown the photograph, Clifford Roberts was asked to identify the wheelbarrow's human cargo: "Oh, hell, that's O.B. Keeler, who sometimes outdid himself at the bar." When asked to elaborate on the circumstances, Roberts explained: "Well, the members decided that when Keeler got in this condition, he was unable to maneuver safely on his own two feet, and so, for the safety of all members, we provided him with this means of transportation."

The wheelbarrow bore a sign, announcing: "This man is a danger to all members when he's drinking, so we've taken a vote to provide him with this safe mode of transportation; and, furthermore, when he's drinking on the premises, we'll be obliged if he uses it!" The object of this good-natured ribbing was a fellow whose heart, the members well knew, was full of youthful enthusiasms and, above all, of kindness.

Keeler played a large role in the formation of the Masters and in attracting the press in the early years. Indeed, he was among the press cabal who coined the title "The Masters" for the tournament, and forced Jones to accept it. His newspaper articles and syndicated columns, along with those of Grantland Rice, William D. Richardson of the *New York Times*, Joe Davis of the *Chicago Tribune*, Alan Gould of the Associated Press, Kerr Petri of the *World Telegram*, and others, did much to spread the word about the new event, and give it credibility. The dear man's affliction, if that's what it was, was shared by the club's founder and about ninety-nine per cent of all the newspapermen and golf writers who ever trod the grounds, and we'll just have a drink on that.

A Sudden Ending

⊷≡》 ○ ○ ○ 《≡⊷

The picture one has of the eleventh hole at the Augusta National Golf Club is of the entrance to a dangerous, though beautiful place. A par four of 445 yards, it begins within a forest, passes through a long, rather narrow corridor onto a rolling hillside, all the while canting from right to left, and falls to a spreading green beside a sinister gathering pond. To the right, a broad, rippling lawn; to the left, the darkening water.

Mounting the hillside, one is fully exposed to the delicious torments of Augusta National's Amen Corner, a sequence of three holes where prayers are never far from the mind. As the 1987 Masters drew to its climax, the farthest thought from anyone's mind was that Larry Mize would choose this setting to perform a miracle.

Mize is a slender, appealing fellow with a fullish swing, rather less than rhythmic for its pause at the top, but one that proceeds easily, without effort. He is long enough and a good iron player, with an assertive touch in the short game. His style is not to show much as he goes along, but there is grit inside. A rising player in 1987, he had not yet crashed through in a big event.

The Masters had been a furious chase that year. Curtis Strange had led after two rounds, and well into the third, until he dumped his second shot into the pond at the fifteenth. Then it was Greg Norman, Roger Maltbie, and Ben Crenshaw drawing ahead, with Bernhard Langer close behind. Within range were Seve Ballesteros, T.C. Chen, and Mize. Well into the fourth round eight players had closed within a stroke of the lead, and at the end it was down to four.

A rash of birdies by Mize on the inward nine, the same from Norman, and then Ballesteros came back with two of his own, and they were all tied with Crenshaw. But Ben bogeyed the seventeenth and was gone, so it would be sudden death among Norman, Ballesteros, and Mize. Seve was eliminated on the tenth, the first playoff hole, crestfallen after missing a short putt and failing to match the pars by Norman and Mize. Now there were two: Norman, the dominant player in the game in 1986, and Mize, the quiet native of Augusta, who had dreamed as a youth of playing in the Masters one day.

They moved to the eleventh, Augusta National's most difficult hole. This had not always been such a menacing hole. Originally, the tee had been placed just to the left of the tenth green, and the hole had played much shorter than it now does. The green in those days was guarded on the left by a wide, shallow bunker, shaped very much in the style of its designer, Alister Mackenzie. Behind the green lay Rae's Creek. After the 1950 Masters, the creek was dammed to create a pond which supplanted the greenside bunker.

In 1951, Sam Snead and Billy "Dynamite" Goodloe both registered eights at this hole after visiting the new pond. They were the first of thousands who would learn about those greenside slopes that draw everything to the water. Then, in 1952, a new tee appeared to the left of the old one, but deeper in the woods which added thirty-five yards to the hole. This was the hole that greeted Norman and Mize in 1987.

Both men drove well. Mize, 194 yards from the hole, played first. Using a five-iron, he pushed the shot onto the lawn beside the green, far away from the hole. From 164 yards, Norman also played to the right, but he reached the edge of the green with a seven-iron. Earlier in the day Mize had played safely to the same lawn and had saved his par, but on that occasion he had been ten yards closer. Now he was forty-six yards from the hole and he well knew the next shot would run quickly on the slick green, which fed everything toward the dreaded pond.

Mize took time to collect himself, then chose his sand iron. He seemed calm as he took his position over the ball, glancing toward the flagstick and the water beyond. The ball flew low, bounced twice before it reached the green, then scurried across the glassy surface, drawn ever closer to the hole. Before anyone realized it would be very close indeed, suddenly it was in. Mize covered his face in disbelief, then leaped and danced on to the green, past the immobile figure of Norman. Greg stood transfixed; it was the second time in less than a year that an upstart had holed out from an impossible position to snatch a major championship from him. There would be no searching response; Mize's shot had struck at his vitals. Norman could still halve the hole, but his putt was never high enough to have a chance.

One could sympathize with Norman's disappointment, but it was one of those occasions when Mize was always going to be the winner. He had driven longer and with greater effect on the tenth than either Norman or Ballesteros, and he had played a better approach than either man. He was cooler and less inclined to force himself into the great business. Watching the drama, one shuddered to think what must have gone through poor Norman's mind as he saw the ball disappear. But there was much to like in the picture of the young man reaching into the most fearful part of the course with this graceful little running shot, and ending things with such a thump.

The Master

--⟩=○ ○ ○ =⟨--

When grizzled veterans gather round to discuss the old masters, the ones who could play any shot and beat any opponent, the names of Hogan and Jones, Snead and Nelson, Player and Palmer come to their minds, but we all know, don't we, that none of these fellows can claim the title, The Master of Augusta. When Bobby Jones made that famous remark about unfamiliarity after watching Jack Nicklaus play golf, he was being partly courteous and partly envious.

What would anyone today say about a man who could safely be predicted to win the Masters, on average, every five or six years for the next thirty? Beginning in 1959, this is more or less what Jack Nicklaus did. When Tiger Woods came along, almost everyone, including Nicklaus, said he "might" exceed this record. And so he might, but Jack actually did it.

Everyone who saw it remembers what a powerful hitter Nicklaus was when he first came out, how he impressed even the resident boomers with his length. "People don't go that far on vacation," said Dave Marr, who was not among them. "They should put a cork in his backside and make him a cannon," said comedian Don Rickles, a golf addict, with insulting accuracy.

A story is told that Nicklaus, going for his first Masters victory in 1963, had reached the thirteenth hole where he uncharacteristically skied his tee shot. Surveying the 260 yards left to the green, he asked his caddie: "Willie, can we get there?" "No sir, Mr. Jack." The Bear continued to stare at the tempting curve of fairway and beckoning green, then hauled out a wood and smashed the ball to the green. As it landed on the distant carpet, his playing partner is said to have muttered to his caddie: "Lord, he's going to run us all off the tour." In a manner of speaking, he did.

After Nicklaus won his third Masters in 1966, his second in a row, Clifford Roberts had seen enough of this and ordered twin bunkers—which he always referred to in the singular—installed at the turn of the eighteenth fairway to prevent Jack from driving too close to the green. Jack scarcely glanced at the new obstacle, teed his ball high and sent it soaring over the bunkers into the old practice field beyond. Child's play.

It was almost inevitable that Roberts and Nicklaus, two of golf's most willful men, would clash, though never in public. In 1967, Jack missed the cut after posting a 79 in the second round and was preparing to leave when Roberts intervened. He was an expert at bullying important people and bending the top stars to his will, even the great Nicklaus. In his halting but stern voice, Roberts informed the defending champion: "Uh, uh, Jack, ahem, uh, we will expect you to stay," delivered with the customary baleful stare. Nicklaus was not at all happy, but Roberts insisted he stay until Sunday to present the green jacket to the winner, and stay he did.

On another occasion, after winning his fifth Masters in 1975, Nicklaus was in town the week prior to the tournament to practice, accompanied by one or two of his staff. At lunch one day, Nicklaus and his chief editorial man, Ken Bowden, were joined by Cliff Roberts. As the sandwiches disappeared, Jack suggested Bowden, a good amateur player, join him for golf that afternoon.

Roberts quickly cleared his throat: "Uh, umm, uh, that'll be just fine, Jack, uh, if you can find a member to play with him." Embarrassed now, Nicklaus said: "You mean, even though I've won five Masters and supposedly am an honorary member, I can't bring a guest?" Cliff stared back: "No, you can't." That was Roberts, and that was that, although a willing member eventually was found and the men played.

People think of Augusta National as a place that favors power hitters, and of course it is, but it's so much more a golf course for thinkers. So what happens when a golfer who combines the power and mental capacity of a Nicklaus meets such a golf course? Oh, about six green jackets that might have been even more because Jack finished second four times and had winning chances in two or three of them.

For all of his power, though, Nicklaus showed himself to be the consummate plodder and plotter. As anyone with a casual interest in the game must know, Jack's ability to think the game through has not been surpassed and probably not equaled, although it led to unforgiveably slow patches of play.

His rivals admired the huge drives and his ability to gouge the ball from deep rough with iron, but not his swing technique. "Jack is not the best ball striker I've ever seen," said Gary Player, "but he has the greatest mind in sports. He never beats himself."

Nicklaus was twenty-three when he won his first Masters in 1963, beating warhorses Sam Snead and Julius Boros and a fast-closing Tony Lema in rough weather. Then, in excellent weather in 1965 when the rivalry with Palmer was at its peak, Jack crushed Arnold and the rest of the field and the golf course, setting a record of 271 that would not be equaled for a dozen years and wouldn't be bettered until 1997, when Tiger Woods finally lowered the mark by one stroke.

Clearly, he could win in any conditions and in winning again in 1966, he became the first repeat winner. On it went until that improbable Masters of 1986 with his son, Jackie, on his bag. When his streak of playing in the major championships slipped into history—following the generation-defying final round 68 and sixth place finish in 1998 at the age of fifty-eight, mind you—it was that one that everybody, including Jack, remembered most fondly.

He has admitted to putting pressure on himself to win each year at Augusta because of his dogged pursuit of the holy grail of professional golf, the capture of four majors in a single year. Only Hogan has approached it with his three in 1953, and Nicklaus was bound to try for it. To have a chance, of course, he must win the Masters and so he went early to Augusta each spring to practice and prepare his game. He has admitted, too, that winning the Masters became too important to him and that he probably lost several as a result.

But who has handled pressure better than he? Where other players approached the back nine at Augusta and grew nervous, experienced dry mouths or twitchy fingers, Nicklaus seemed to grow calmer. His pulse slowed, his focus intensified, and he actually played better under pressure than he normally did, which was itself a high standard.

His primary weapons, apart from the length and the piston-like putting stroke, have been his focus, intelligence, preparation, analytic ability, and voracious appetite for the big moment. Another mark of the Nicklaus game has always been how very conservatively he played. Unlike so many of his rivals, he rarely hit a shot without having a safe bailout in mind. It was a mark of his patience, and a monumental patience it must have been, that he was willing to play this way when, with that power, he could so easily have been tempted to overwhelm the game.

The story of the 1986 Masters has been told too often to bear repeating, except for this. It was a tournament that Seve Ballesteros lost on that last day when his four iron went into the pond at fifteen. Seve led by four until that fateful stroke, but emerged with bogey. Nicklaus, at age forty-six, was on a tear and eating up strokes; he had eagled the same hole earlier, and all but holed his tee shot on sixteen. Was the relentless charge noticed by others? Did pressure from Nicklaus find the emotional Spaniard as he swung? Does a Bear rule the fairways of the Augusta National?

What is so clear to us now, and was even then, is that when the opportunities came, Nicklaus was mentally prepared to capitalize on the slightest flinch or weakness in another's game. He was ready to take advantage of that, and, more than anyone else, hadn't the least fear of doing so. There was none that day, either, only the pure satisfaction such a triumph at such an age in such company and at such a place could give the greatest player in the game. He may not have been a master of all the shots, but Jack Nicklaus was the master of himself and, in this simple old game, that is usually enough.

The Glory Hole

—→══○ ○ ○ ○ ══←—

With all due respect, the fifteenth hole at the Augusta National should be stuffed, glassed over, and locked away in the Smithsonian Institution. Not that there is anything wrong with the hole, mind you, but how do you play in a museum?

A par-five of 520 yards with a broad pond stretched across the front of its green, Augusta's fifteenth is a repository of historic golf shots: Gene Sarazen's double-eagle in 1935; Doug Ford's spoon second to set up birdie and key his victory in 1957; Curtis Strange's mighty splash after a misplayed second in 1985; Fuzzy Zoeller's even mightier splash over the green and into the pond by the sixteenth; Bob Goalby's majestic three-iron for eagle in 1968; Jumbo Ozaki's operatic eleven after dumping three balls in the pond in 1987, a record score on this hole; Seve Ballesteros's sickening four-iron that fluttered into the water in 1986; Chip Beck's inglorious layup in 1993; Jose Maria Olazabal's magnificent clutch putt for eagle in 1995; the mammoth drives of Nicklaus and Weiskopf, now unimaginably eclipsed by the low earth orbits of Tiger Woods. The hole is a shrine of famous and infamous feats. You cannot find a place to stand where someone hasn't played a legendary stroke. Not even in the water.

When he won the 1947 Masters, Jimmy Demaret played a shot from the pond in front of the green that today would be replayed on television screens around the world. Playing from shallow water is not particularly difficult for professional golfers, but this pond isn't shallow and its banks are steep. In going for the green with his second shot, Demaret had carried the pond, but his ball hit into the bank above it, rolled back, and disappeared beneath the water.

Demaret crossed to the far side and peered into the lagoon. Seeing nothing alive, he removed a shoe and one sock and rolled up his trousers. He placed his right leg into the water, then climbed back ashore to remove the other shoe and sock. His playing companion was Byron Nelson, who wondered if Demaret's piano-leg-shaped legs would support his sturdy frame as he clambered back, both feet now in the water. The slope was just as steep under the water, and slippery. The ball was fairly deep and could easily slide deeper. Under the rules, Demaret could not probe its depth or ground his club in the hazard.

"I'll be careful," said Demaret. He did not think to add marvelous. Jimmy Demaret had probably the best hands in the game, strong and thick, but with a feathery touch. With one foot in the water now, and one foot out, he drew the club back and then drove it into the water, well behind the ball. The wedge vanished, splashing both water and the ball forward. The ball fairly glittered as it rose from the water and came to rest four feet from the hole. Jimmy holed the putt for birdie and went on to a 69, sharing the first round lead with Nelson.

Even though the stroke was played in the first round, it was an extraordinary one and gave him a great push toward winning. He shot four under par over the next three rounds and finished with a score of 281. The two strokes he saved on the fifteenth were just the margin he needed to hold off Nelson and

Frank Stranahan, who tied for second at 283. This was Demaret's second Masters victory. He had won in 1940, and he
would win again in 1950, becoming the first person to win
three.

In the final round that year, over the course he had built,
Bobby Jones scored 80, the first time he had shot this high in
the Masters. Jones had begun to feel the effects of his sad illness
and would play only once more, in 1948, before the disease laid
him low. Jones was more than the creator of the place—he was
the reason all the best players in the game wanted to play there,
especially the younger ones eager to prove themselves.

Through the 1990s, this privileged preserve has had five cura-
tors: Clifford Roberts, Bill Lane, Hord Hardin, Jack Stephens,
and, most recently, the delightfully nicknamed William
"Hootie" Johnson. If early one morning Johnson should wander
out to the fifteenth and find one of those youngsters lurking
among the trees, glancing speculatively at the branches, he
needn't be worried. The fellow is probably looking for glory, and
a place to hit one of those shots that belong in the museum.

A Select Company

A small cottage industry has grown up around the Masters that owes its existence to one of the Augusta National's oldest traditions, the right to do things its own way. The original name of the tournament, remember, was the Annual Invitational Tournament, and invitational means you must wait to be invited. It also means that you might be uninvited, should the occasion arise, and it has. Several times, in fact, even among select members of the press corps who were otherwise courted by the chairman, Clifford Roberts, and who, in turn, almost to a man, revered the founder, Bobby Jones.

From the club's earliest days, Cliff Roberts carefully cultivated the press with a strategy that drew on Bob Jones's warm, southern charm backed by Roberts's own flinty resolution. Both men understood how important the press would be to the tournament's success, but neither was inclined to indulge a careless word that might possibly cast the tournament or the club itself in a bad light. As the years went by, the press corps changed and grew larger just as the country did.

Attitudes and customs changed, and so did language and its

vernacular. When Jack Whitaker uttered his famous on-air remark in 1966, innocently describing the Masters patrons who were spilling across the eighteenth fairway as a "mob," Cliff Roberts was incensed and arranged to have Whitaker dropped from the CBS broadcasting crew for future Masters.

Jack Whitaker's is probably the richest, most professional voice to have covered golf on radio and television and Jack himself is among the game's finest essayists and historians. He has an extraordinary ability, something of a legend in the business, to gather his thoughts in a few moments, then turn to the camera without notes and deliver as eloquent a summation of the tournament as you will read in any magazine.

So, when Whitaker was fired, people noticed. Roberts had not seemed to react so decisively to newspaper reporters, however. Zeke Wood, sports editor of the *Augusta Herald*, for example, wrote a column in 1957 in which he described Ben Hogan's gallery crawling "stealthily across the seventeenth fairway like a herd of South American driver ants." Not a peep was heard from Cliff Roberts. There were other examples of a loose vernacular appearing in the print medium, suggesting that a higher standard may have been applied by the club to the phrases used by television commentators.

In recent years, the dismissals of Ben Wright, who had stirred up a hornet's nest away from the Masters with comments about the sexual preferences of women golfers, and of Gary McCord, whose irreverent reference to "bikini wax" in 1994 in connection with the Augusta National's putting surfaces had earned another summary exit, drew even more attention. "I was very upset with McCord," said Whitaker with a straight face. "I had been a member of the most exclusive club in sports, and now he's ruined it."

These incidents, titillating though they were, did nothing to jeopardize the relationship between CBS and the Masters. Before them, however, one episode almost did. It involved Heywood Hale Broun, another gifted television essayist, and Robert Wood, then the president of Columbia Broadcasting System.

"Woody" Broun's pieces on tennis, golf, horse racing, and other topics appeared regularly on the CBS Network during the '60s and '70s. However, Broun was a member of the CBS News Division, not CBS Sports. In 1975, he was assigned to narrate a segment about Lee Elder's first appearance in the Masters. Clifford Roberts turned down his application for press credentials, perhaps anticipating Broun's probing ironies and social commentary in a time of racial unrest.

So, the resourceful Broun donned a disguise and stood in front of Augusta National's front gate to narrate his piece, occasionally peering through the bushes as he did. Then, clad in a trench coat and armed with a broom, he followed behind a garbage truck as it drove into the club's grounds, describing the entry on camera as "an armored invasion." The segment ran on Sunday evening as part of a Mike Wallace piece, and drew sufficient comment the following day that Cliff Roberts contacted Robert Wussler, president of CBS Sports, and tried to get Woody Broun fired.

To placate Cliff Roberts, Bob Wussler apparently, and rather quickly if the story is to be believed, agreed to Roberts's demand. The next day reports in the press appeared stating that Broun had been dismissed and an apology tendered to the Augusta National. But the reports were untrue. In those days, network news divisons were all-powerful and, it follows, independent. Robert Wood, president of CBS, decided that the network could not be influenced by the request, nor would it consider firing Broun.

Who can tell what Cliff Roberts's response to this may have been? Broun has said that Bob Wood gave Roberts a choice of paying CBS for the cost of the permanent cables installed for the Masters (estimated cost in the neighborhood of $200,000), or closing the course for a week so that CBS could dig them up.

Frank Chirkinian, then the producer of the Masters telecast, denies this happened.

In any event, no apologies were offered, CBS kept the Masters and Broun his job. Later, when Heywood Hale Broun retired, he wrote to CBS chairman William Paley thanking him "for not firing me, and for risking his round of golf with Ike at Augusta National." With a classical education and an ear for the well-turned phrase, Woody Broun published a book of stories in 1977 whose title, *Tumultuous Merriment*, was taken from Samuel Johnson's not-so-approving description of sports and games.

Whitaker was reinstated by CBS and the Masters in 1973, after several years of exile, though he eventually departed to join ABC. Jack still broadcasts for ABC and ESPN and adds his graceful essays to one or two golf magazines. McCord continues his work with CBS, though he and Wright still serve their banishments from the Augusta National, one imposed by the Masters, and one not. Together, these men form a select company whose names are associated, however fleetingly, with the grand tournament that comes to us on television in early April each year.

The Astonishing
Player

❖❧ ○ ○ ○ ❧❖

When we pause to look back at the past century of golf, which won't be long now, the most astonishing fellow of all the great ones from Vardon to Woods may prove to have been the fierce little South African, Gary Player. He must be. Possessing an ungainly swing, lacking real power, and with only his unconquerable tenacity and a vastly underrated putting stroke to save him, Player has surpassed all but a handful of men who have played the game. Not Paul Runyan, nor Jerry Barber, nor Doug Ford, nor today's Paul Azinger has achieved more with less obvious physical gifts.

Looking at him, one wonders how he has managed to assemble his record of nine major championships and two hundred titles worldwide, all the while needing a Charles Atlas brochure and a small ladder to meet his rivals on equal terms. Week after week, year after year, decade after decade, Gary Player has kept coming, and if we're not paying attention, he'll soon pass Sam Snead and Gene Sarazen for longevity. With his insatiable quest for distance, Player disdained classical style and instead developed his familiar slashing moves in the long game, golf swings that sent his legs scurrying from under him in a furious effort to maintain his balance. As a consequence, Gary frequently put himself in the most difficult positions, much like his keen rival, Arnold Palmer. Almost unnoticed, though, Player would escape them using the same bold style as his friend, though perhaps not as breathtaking because of the immense power of Palmer's attack.

Just when we were ready to write off Player as a contender in the majors, here he came to claim another. It was bad enough that he won a Masters title on a course that did not, at first glance, suit him. He was, after all, the first foreign player to win a green jacket. But, then he won two. Well, that's it for Gary, we thought, and so he returned at the age of forty-two to collect his third Masters in 1978. He began the last round seven shots behind the leader, and when he reached the ninth hole, he was still out of the hunt. No one paid him much notice because nearly everyone forgot something about him, and about golf.

Gary Player is the most optimistic, positive thinker in the game, and believes himself capable of anything. Moreover, he is most dangerous when cornered, as he has shown so often. That alone makes him an infuriating opponent. Just when you think you have him, he wriggles free. Shots over willow trees and holed bunker shots are nothing to this fellow. Drive a stake in his heart and he will slowly rise to sink his fangs in your throat. The man just doesn't give up. If we had his attitude, any of us could knock ten strokes from our handicaps.

Golf is finally a mental, not a physical game, isn't it? Bobby Jones wrote about this quite a lot, and could find no technical explanation for why or when the wand touched a Sarazen or a Hagen, or even himself. There was no formula, the outcome never certain. A fellow might want the prize too badly, be too determined, or concentrate too much, paths that led to uncertain ends; but, if he failed to apply himself, he might be lost entirely. That's the real game, as Jones and Hagen and Ford and Player well understood.

The wand touched Gary Player as he stood on the ninth tee that Sunday in 1978. He birdied seven of the remaining ten holes and posted a score of 64, which included a record-tying 30 on the back nine. Hubert Green, the leader after three rounds, had a chance to tie Gary's four-round total of 277, but missed a three-footer at the last to finish a stroke behind in a tie with Tom Watson and Rod Funseth.

The late golf writer, Dick Taylor, used to remind us that Player had been motivated, in part, by a newspaper story from the previous week's Greensboro Open, which described Gary as "a fading star." His tour rivals might have preferred to let the sleeping badger lie. Other quotes would irritate the five-foot-seven South African, who later told *Golf Digest's* Ross Goodner: "Robert Trent Jones said I'm an unlikely winner because my muscles get tied up with all that exercise. What crap! Just like his golf courses!"

When the press cheered him for winning the Masters at the "advanced" age of forty-two, Gary replied in all earnestness: "I'll be playing world-class golf when I'm fifty because proper diet and exercise keep my body young." An understatement. At sixty-one, he won his third Senior British Open at Royal Portrush in Ireland, opening and closing the tournament with bookend 68s and running home a fifteen-foot birdie putt to win in a playoff, beating men a dozen years his junior. Then in 1998, at age sixty-two, he became the oldest player to make the cut in the Masters, and late that summer won yet another PGA Senior tournament, his nineteenth.

As he's happy to point out, Player has beaten the best golfers of three separate eras—Hogan's, the one of Nicklaus and Palmer, and Watson's. He still has that devastating putting stroke, delivered with a sharp punch, and the deadliest wedge and sand game since Sam Snead's. Gary once promised to hang it up after playing in the millennial Open at St. Andrews in the year 2000. Somehow, we doubt it; he'll only be sixty-four, you know.

One That Got Away

✦⭄ ∘ ∘ ∘ ⭅✦

There are times you know beyond doubt the universe is indifferent to the plight of puny man. Life is peppered with examples of hopes gone wrong, luck turned bad, justice lost. Golf is the perfect game for experiencing this sort of thing on a regular basis, and we all do, don't we? How much worse it must be for the great players who can command their shots with such majestic certainty, yet who falter just like the rest of us.

Next to the magical finish in 1986 when Jack Nicklaus proved what everyone already knew, that he is superhuman, the Masters people recall with perhaps the most poignance is the one in 1979. One of the finest young men in golf was on his way to claiming a green jacket after setting a torrid pace through three rounds. The young gentleman was Ed Sneed, a native of Roanoke, Virginia, who had gone on to attend Ohio State in Columbus and, after graduating, had taken up residence there.

Sneed had won three official tournaments up to that point in his career, and had been chosen for the 1977 Ryder Cup team, but had given no evidence that he might win at Augusta National. In 1979, however, he tore the place apart in the first three rounds with scores of 68-67-69, twelve under par. Sneed led the field by five strokes as he moved to the first tee on Sunday. "Coming into the Masters, I'd been playing as well as I ever had," said Sneed. "I had just finished second to Tom Watson at Hilton Head, and my confidence was very high."

Sneed played a practice round with Ken Venturi on the Sunday before the tournament, and Venturi had shown Ed a new shot with his pitching wedge. "He taught me how to play a soft draw to hidden pins, a shot of which Kenny is a master. We talked about where to hit some of the longer shots so as to leave proper distance for these wedge shots, and I followed the plan."

The Masters galleries and millions on television watched Sneed's performance unfold with delight and a bit of awe at his mastery of his own game. That's why these fellows are called "masters," isn't it, and this is the place they're confirmed, isn't it? So, when the great disaster struck on Sunday, no one could quite grasp it, nor wanted to, least of all Sneed himself.

Ed Sneed first saw the course in 1974. He had driven from the tournament at Hilton Head and arrived at the Augusta National Sunday evening just before dark. "I asked the manager, Phil Wahl, if I could go out and see the course for a few minutes, and he said it was okay. I just walked out the back of the clubhouse in my street shoes, and was overcome. I went down to the first tee, the ninth green, the eighteenth, then over to the tenth hole. I ran down the tenth fairway all the way past the green, and never stopped until I got to the eleventh green. It was six or six-thirty at night, and I was pumped.

"I walked over to the twelfth, and up thirteen, and on; by the time I reached sixteen, it was getting dark. I walked up the eighteenth in the darkness, and remember my first impression being how small the green looked, compared with how it looked on television. I kept waiting for a Pinkerton guard to come out of the trees and arrest me. My new loafers were all wet, but I remember being exhilarated just to be there. I was out the next morning at 8:30 a.m. to play a practice round all by myself."

All week the weather was good, but Sunday was a blustery day, with winds gusting to fifteen to twenty miles per hour. "It made the course tougher, but I was kind of glad, in a way, that it wasn't one of those days where someone could shoot 64 or 65," said Sneed. He had made only one bogey in three rounds, and looked confident as he drove from the first tee. "I knew where I was, and I had led tournaments before," said Sneed. "I thought I could do it." The wind picked up strength as the day wore on, pushing scores up. Only two men shot 69, Nicklaus and North, and one, Zoeller, a 70.

After bogeys at four and six, Sneed grazed the cup at seven, rimmed out a fifteen-footer at eight, both of which would have given him birdies, then faced one of those cliff-hangers at the ninth green. "I was twenty feet above the hole, and hit an unbelievable putt," said Sneed. "I barely tapped the ball; it trickled and trickled down the slope, and just lipped out. I don't know how it stayed out of the hole." Three pars that could have been birdies. His lead was shrinking, too.

The pressure was beginning to tell. Sneed hit a heavy approach at ten, and came up short. A bogey, then a brave six-footer to save par at eleven and he still led by one. The flagstick at twelve was back right, as it always is on Sunday, and Ed stroked an "easy six-iron." Too much club. His ball hit on the knob behind the green, and plugged into the back bunker. "I was fighting every hole now, fighting myself, fighting to hold myself together," said Sneed. "I thought seriously about playing away from the hole. I had kept to my plan every round, and avoided the water all week. Finally, I told myself, 'To hell with this! Just hit a decent bunker shot and give yourself a chance at par.' I splashed it from a fried-egg lie, and almost holed it. The ball stopped six inches from the cup."

The par kept him in the lead, and he hit a fine drive at the thirteenth, Augusta National's most provocative hole. "That bunker shot turned me around. All of a sudden, I felt it again. I had about two hundred yards to the green, and wanted to go for it, but I had an awkward stance and a marginal lie. It took all my composure to put the long club back in my bag and lay up with a seven-iron." The ball ran down the left side, leaving Sneed a perfect angle into the flag. He pitched to within four feet, and made birdie.

After a par at fourteen, where Watson had bogeyed, Ed moved two strokes in front. Ahead of him, Watson and Zoeller both birdied fifteen. "At that point, Zoeller was a stroke behind Watson, and, in my mind, I was playing against Watson," said Sneed. "I've always looked at scoreboards, so I knew exactly where I stood." A birdie followed at fifteen, after laying up with his second. "I couldn't get there in two; the wind was too strong," said Sneed, who then hit a beautiful wedge approach, just as Venturi had showed him, and holed a six-footer for birdie to go ahead by three.

In a practice round with Tom Weiskopf, Tom's caddie, Leroy Shultz, had watched Sneed hit a shot to within two feet of the hole, cut in the back left, at the sixteenth. "Eddie, if you hit one like that on Sunday, you sure can make 'em holler," said Leroy. On Sunday, Sneed stroked a four-iron into the wind toward the right side of the green, another masterful stroke. The ball hopped once and started rolling down the hill toward the hole, but then stopped. "As I walked to the green, I kept looking at the ball, wondering why it didn't roll to the bottom of the slope. When I marked the ball, I found it resting in a pitch-mark that hadn't been repaired." Sneed replaced his ball in the divot and ran the putt four feet by, then missed coming back.

Now he was two strokes ahead, and, after a perfect drive at seventeen, he had about 120 yards to the hole. "I took a pitching wedge and cut the legs off it; the ball landed twenty feet short of the flag and just ran to the back, a yard or so off the putting surface. The putt hit the edge of the hole, but went three feet past, and I missed the next." Bogey, and now he was one stroke in front coming to the eighteenth.

Sneed cut a three-wood to the center of the fairway, and had 160 yards left. He aimed a seven-iron to the right side of the green, intending to draw the ball, but came off the shot slightly. The ball landed short, bounced ten feet in the air and went dead right, finishing at the edge of the bunker. The wind had blown sand around the area, an unneeded distraction, but he hit a solid chip. "It was the hardest shot I had all day," said Sneed. "I picked it clean, using a sand wedge, and the ball ran to within six or seven feet of the hole. I played the putt to go a little right, but it didn't. It rolled slowly over the left edge, and hung over the hole." Another bogey, and now he was tied with Watson and Zoeller, both of whom had closed strongly.

Three holes, three lost shots, and now a playoff. "After those three bogeys, the tendency is to get down on yourself, to lose your focus," said Sneed. "But, I didn't. The officials told me I could go to the clubhouse and take whatever time I needed, but I said, 'No, I'd just like a little drink of water.' I told myself the tournament was not over. At ten, we all hit good shots, and made pars.

"At eleven, Fuzzy hit a big, slinging hook that went a long way. Watson and I were close together, and I played first, hitting a five-iron from 186 yards. It almost hit the flag, carrying just past and running into the bunker. Watson hit his to about twenty feet, Zoeller to about twelve. My bunker shot lipped the cup; I thought it was going in. After Watson missed, Fuzzy made his, becoming the first man since Sarazen to win in his first Masters appearance."

Sneed's judgment and strategy had been impeccable all day; he had taken the correct line at thirteen, fifteen, and sixteen, and had birdied the two par-fives. He was brave and resolute at every turn. Only his luck and his nerve failed him at the end—

the freak pitch-mark at sixteen, and the shaky irons at the last two holes. "I tightened up and lost my game in the middle of the round, but I fought through it, and the bunker shot at twelve revitalized me. The wheels never came off. I know what happens inside you when things go wrong. There have been times when I've recovered, and times when I haven't. I did recover at Augusta; I just didn't win."

No, and a pity he didn't. The Masters lost an attractive winner whose appeal in defeat seemed to muffle our momentary lust for celebrity and tinsel. "I thought that was as hard as the game can be to a man, even more so than Norman in 1996," said Dave Marr. "When he put the ball safely on the green at sixteen, I thought he'd won, but then we watched it slowly get peeled away." Did anyone need to be reminded that it's a grand, but cruel game?

The Miracle at
Rae's Creek

⊰⊱ ∘ ∘ ∘ ⊰⊱

The exquisite torments and distractions of the short twelfth might fill a book, and they nearly have. The combination of creek, forest, and wind has seldom been better matched in a golf hole, and we sometimes wonder how it came about. Was the creation of this little par-three a mad accident, an act of wanton serendipity, or was it due to the combined guile of Alister Mackenzie and his coconspirator, Bobby Jones?

Somewhere in golfing scripture it is written that "a great course will yield to a great round of golf," and, we might similarly say, a great hole to a great stroke. That seems fair enough, and it's true that Claude Harmon, Bill Hyndman, and Curtis Strange scored aces here; but the truth is the twelfth hole yields to miracles more than anything else. In 1952 standing on the tee in the final round, Sam Snead looked a certain winner. Into the creek in one, a drop into a depression in two, into the shaggy bank below the green in three. A six perhaps? No; Sam's next found the bottom of the hole, and the bogey four kept him well free of the pack all the way to the winner's table.

The previous year, Snead's great nemesis, Lew Worsham, had done him one better. Worsham, nicknamed "Chin" for his most prominent anatomical feature, had stolen a U.S. Open title from Snead in St. Louis when he called for a measurement as Sam was preparing to putt on the last green of their playoff in 1947. Both balls lay about a yard from the hole. The measurement showed that Snead was, indeed, away, but he missed, and Worsham holed, a pretty act of gamesmanship against one of golf's greatest gamesmen.

In the final round of the 1951 Masters, Worsham's tee shot at the twelfth hit the water, but bounced out and ran onto the green. He holed the putt for what was probably the most miraculous birdie in the tournament's history. A sportswriter of the time said: "Worsham's feat may have been the only time in a major championship when a player hit into the water and came out with a two."

Though nearly miraculous, these shots can be explained by the laws of physics. Some cannot; the tournament would wait until 1992 to witness a proper miracle. The bank above Rae's Creek in 1952 was covered with long tangles of unkempt grass, which saved Snead's ball from rolling back into the creek. By the 1980s, the bank had been groomed and polished and the grass shaved to within a quarter-inch of its roots, all in the name of the golf course's appearance on television. Clifford Roberts had decreed the place to be manicured, and so it was.

Since then, balls landing on this bank kissed the ground, and quickly vanished. There was nothing to stop them from rolling straight back into the creek. Everyone knew it. Contestants, officials, spectators, little children, people watching on television who understood little of golf knew it: When a contestant's ball lands on the bank below the twelfth green, it's a bath for him. The roster of those victimized by the slippery bank excludes practically no one among Masters contestants: Tom Weiskopf, Sandy Lyle, Greg Norman, Jack Nicklaus, Payne Stewart, and dozens more have suffered the indignity.

So, when Freddie Couples lofted one of his high floating iron shots to the same spot in 1992, everyone knew its fate. Or thought they did. Couples arrived at the twelfth hole on Sunday with a slender lead over his friend and sometimes mentor, Raymond Floyd. Choosing an eight-iron, Fred aimed at the middle of the green, and swung. "I never looked at the flag over there on the right, but there's something in my body that swings where the pin is, and, sure enough, I blocked the shot," said Couples afterward.

The ball hit the bank four feet above Rae's Creek, and rolled back, just as everyone knew it would. But then it stopped. It lay there nestled in the turf, a foot or so from the water while Fred made his way across the bridge, scarcely believing his luck and wondering with all of us how long the ball would stay. If it hadn't been recorded on instant replay, who would have believed it? "I've never seen a ball stop there," said Couples. Wasting little time, he pitched up the bank to within a foot of the hole, and tapped in for his par. A sigh of relief from a few million viewers on television, and surely from Freddie himself.

Only once before in memory had a ball stopped on this bank. In the stormy Masters of 1936, Tommy Armour and Walter Hagen came to this little hole made nearly unplayable by a violent, two-day deluge that had swollen the creek. Armour was known far and wide as the "Iron Master" for his skill with those clubs, and this time he lofted his shot gently and safely over the water onto the green. Sir Walter played one of his low windcheaters, hoping to fool the fickle gusts, but the ball fell short, hit into the bank, and stuck. It was saved only because the bank was covered with thick, untended clumps of grass which stopped the ball's progress; today, it would meet oblivion.

Fred Couples went on to finish the 1992 Masters in fine form, winning by two strokes from Floyd, who was trying for his second Masters victory. Raymond hit a miracle shot of his own at the fourteenth on Sunday; using a sand club from a yard short of the green, he chipped his ball forty-five feet across that great rumpled surface and it ran into the hole. Later, Couples admitted he was skittish at the twelfth. "It was the most nervous I've ever felt," said Freddie. "All kinds of things were racing through my mind." Almost everything except that miracle we think we saw.

But Freddie repeated his ridiculous party trick in 1998, credible evidence that he's in communion with the troll who dwells beneath the little bridge there. It was too much to credit coincidence when he put his tee shot in the same spot and the ball again stayed on the bank in that Masters he all but won. Of course, the troll had its revenge at the next hole, the last of the trio at Amen Corner. At the thirteenth on Sunday, Fred visited the forest and then Rae's Creek and was given his just deserts, the double bogey that cost him a second Masters title.

Forty Million

-⊶≡》 ○ ○ ○ 《≡⊷-

For much of the decade leading up to his dreadful collapse in the 1996 Masters, Greg Norman was frequently nominated by his peers the best player in the game and "the man to beat" in the major championships. His competitive record through this period was superb, though not supreme, but his performances in the major championships and other events from 1984 onward suggest he was never the man to beat so much as a man who would beat himself.

As the tournaments and seasons slipped by, it began to occur to people that Greg Norman was an easy mark on the grand occasions; just ask Bob Tway, Larry Mize, Fuzzy Zoeller, David Frost, Mark Calcavecchia, Jim Gallagher, Corey Pavin, Paul Azinger, and Nick Faldo. All you had to do was get him to the final round, or put him on a truly testing course like Olympic or Shinnecock Hills or Pebble Beach or Oakland Hills, and he turned to mush. Norman himself would say as much, although his eyes would flash murder.

What a hard judgment this is, for Norman has been the most attractive and dynamic character in the game almost since he arrived in the early 1980s. He could with justice claim to be the longest, straight driver since Cary Middlecoff, a dazzling iron player, and the owner of a beautiful touch in the short game, including one of the best putting strokes in the game. What, then, goes wrong? Norman is the sad but living proof of golf's bitterest truth—that the game is played so much more with our interior rather than our exterior selves.

This is most apparent at Augusta National because its features, designed with subtle intent and guile by, in Crenshaw's words, the most cerebral golfer in history, so easily encourage and so starkly punish the feeble attempt at the end. None of us has wished it to be true of Norman and, indeed, golf's legions have continued to cheer him on. His commercial successes have been enormous and have compensated, no doubt. But, for so gallant and popular a figure, these must be ghastly substitutes for the lost endings.

It's always tempting to blame the Fates for one's misfortunes, but the truth is that Norman has written the story himself. In golf, it is not the moving finger that writes, but ourselves, and that's why it is the game it is. Norman's great failures have been colossal not only because he has been favored to win so often, nor because of the occasions themselves, but for his own missteps. Tragedies do not occur in golf tournaments, unless you count lightning strikes, but wrecks do. Norman's have not been limited to the Masters, although heaven knows this tournament has provided the setting for several he might rather forget.

There was the Mize shocker in 1987, and others, but in 1996 Greg finally had put the genie back in the bottle. After a decade of near-misses, he had marched three rounds in commanding style, including a majestic 63 the opening day, and had taken a six-stroke lead into Sunday's final round. Of course, we should have known he had no chance whatsoever because this was the Masters and we all know what happens on Sundays at Augusta, and we all knew that the fellow leading at twelve-under was Greg Norman, and we knew about him, too.

Joining Norman on the first tee for that final round was Nick Faldo, who was seven-under-par but might just as well have been along for background music for all the chance he was given. We might have noticed, had we bothered, that Nick already had two Masters titles in his cupboard and was the most calculating and disciplined player since Hogan: Faldo would play a four iron to the widest runway at O'Hare, and resist any reasonable temptation if he thought it to his strategic advantage.

In nearly perfect weather that Sunday, Faldo picked his way carefully around the front nine in thirty-four strokes while Norman was taking thirty-eight. Cracks had appeared in Greg's game early in the round, but his biggest misstep came at the ninth. After a huge drive, he was left with ninety-eight yards up the hill to the sloping green, but his approach fell short and pulled back off the green. A bogey, and Norman's lead was down to two, which surely gave heart to Faldo.

Two more bogeys by Greg at the next two holes, and the lead was gone. At twelve, Faldo made a careful par while Norman found the water and holed in five. The rest is too painful to describe, though millions watched the gruesome drama unfold on television. It was like water torture, slow and of a horrid certainty. When a desperate chip for eagle at the fifteenth ran by the hole, Greg fell to the ground, the last spark of hope extinguished. Back in the clubhouse, the players' locker room grew silent. "You could have cut the tension with a knife; nobody could believe what was happening," said his friend, Nick Price.

On the day, Norman made five bogeys and two doubles to finish with 78; Faldo toured the back in 33 and ended with a flourish, holing for three at the last for a round of 67. It was reminiscent of Casper's final round at Olympic in 1966, and, like his, was a masterful round by a master golfer. Faldo had beaten his man by eleven strokes that day, and had won by five. At the last green, Faldo embraced his rival and murmured words of sympathy. Nick had tasted defeat in a major, too, but not at Augusta when his chances had come, and never so bitter. Greg was as gracious in defeat as was Faldo in victory. He offered no excuses save his own mistakes, and told the press: "It's not the end of the world," then added, "My life will continue. I've got forty million bucks." No mystery there.

The mighty Aussie has reached very close to the pinnacle of golf. We sense that he belongs in that select group of green-jacketed Masters winners; even the press has pulled for him and wished him there. But it hasn't happened, and no one knows better than he that you can't finagle your way into the plush seats with wishes or honeyed words or fancy press clippings. He is a staunch sportsman who accepts golf's uncertain outcomes, a man who has stood up to adversity and its companion, defeat, as bravely as anyone could.

Greg Norman was forty-three when the 1998 Masters took place. His return in 1997 had been mercifully overshadowed by the sensational performance of Tiger Woods, and here he was again, though not as a favorite. Not many writers gave Norman a chance to win in his mid-forties, although his immense powers seemed hardly diminished. Sam Snead, Ben Hogan, Gary Player, Jack Nicklaus, Ben Crenshaw had all won Masters titles in their forties, so why not Norman? We could only point to the black Fates when he missed the cut, then underwent shoulder surgery a few weeks later.

Perhaps the shoulder condition had contributed to his uneven performances in recent years, or perhaps the edge had already been taken from his game by repeated disappointments, although if Norman were to come back at the age of forty-six or fifty to win at Augusta we should all be counted perfect clods for writing these horrid things about him.

Ben's Partner

Can anyone doubt that golf is most often a game of emotion? For most players, it is a vexing battle to control one's emotion under the stress of competition. The professionals devise a thousand ways to subdue their emotions, to keep them on an even keel week after week, year after year. Hogan's stare; Trevino's chatter; Parnevik's hat; Langer's snail's pace; Zoeller's whistle, and the cast-iron mentality of a Nicklaus or a Casper. Those who succeed in doing so are the most consistent, and usually the most successful, as professional players.

But it's not always so. Occasionally we witness exceptions to the rule, and one such time came in the 1995 Masters when Ben Crenshaw won his second green jacket. His performance that year on the professional tour had been desultory, neither overcoming his long game deficiencies nor exhibiting his customary magic with the wand. Crenshaw without his putting, as his peers well know, is an ordinary customer.

Leading up to the Masters that year, his putting was, well, ordinary. The Sunday before the tournament, Ben's mentor and teacher from childhood, Harvey Penick, had passed away at the age of ninety. Crenshaw and Tom Kite, Penick's star pupils, had returned to Austin, Texas, to serve as pallbearers at Harvey's funeral. For Crenshaw, a man of deep emotional strains whose feelings for the history and traditions of the game animate his life as a golfer, something snapped into place. He returned to Augusta bearing what, to most, seemed an unbearable burden.

After an opening round of 70, when Jack Nicklaus at age fifty-five fired a 67 to stand a stroke from the lead, Ben Crenshaw at age forty-three shot his own 67 the second day to climb within two strokes of the leader, Jay Haas, who had blistered the course in 64. After Saturday's third round, Ben was tied for the lead at ten under par on a day when seven different players led or shared the lead at one time or other. His coleader was Brian Henninger, who was making his first Masters appearance.

Ben seemed almost calm amid the tumult that accompanies a major tournament and the emotional aftermath of Penick's funeral. There was a look of quiet determination about him that we had not seen before. "I think I was determined to hang on for dear life," Crenshaw said. "My concentration never wavered, perhaps that was what people saw." His caddie, Carl Jackson, had offered two simple tips at the beginning of the week: to move the ball back in his stance a little, because Crenshaw's tendency is to "scoot the ball forward, at times," and to make a tighter shoulder turn "because my arms were separating from my body on the backswing."

Just as Harvey Penick's teaching had been kept simple, so were these offerings, and Crenshaw was reminded of his old friend's gentle admonitions: "Take dead aim, and trust your swing," Harvey had repeated year after year. Of such simple thoughts are tranquil golf swings born. Crenshaw's was as tranquil as it had ever been, and his confidence was beginning to match his determination. The putting stroke? Don't ask; he managed the four rounds without a single three-putt green.

Ben's final round of 68 was too good for Davis Love III, who closed with 66 to finish one stroke behind the winner. As the shadows began lengthening on Sunday, Crenshaw survived Amen Corner and reached the final stretch of holes and found birdies waiting at the sixteenth and seventeenth. A little putt of five feet at sixteen, after a splendid six iron, followed by a Crenshaw specialty at seventeen where he holed a fourteen-footer that curled several inches to the right as it hunted the hole. "As pretty a putt as I've ever hit," said Ben afterward.

Now it was on to the eighteenth. "That birdie at seventeen took the pressure off, and I hit a good drive at eighteen," said Crenshaw. "As I walked up the hill, I was thinking, 'I can't believe this is about to happen.' I started breaking on that eight-iron second shot; my concentration was breaking up, I wasn't totally committed to it, and sort of rushed the swing." The ball fell short, and two more strokes brought it to within a few feet of the hole. A moment later, his fifth stroke fell in the hole and Crenshaw nearly fell in on top of it. "It was all welling up within me, and how I held up for that final putt I don't know," said Ben. "That's when I just had to let the floodgates go. It was overwhelming."

His caddie, Carl Jackson, reached out to hold him as Ben's body went limp and his arms folded across his head. Overlooked in all the emotion was the fact that Crenshaw's 274 was the third best score in Masters history. To have finished as he did, holding himself together at the end with the refrains of the departed Penick as background music can be seen as one of the bravest, most emotional in Masters history. I suppose if the multitudes hadn't been there to see it, no one would believe such a tale.

"That victory still gives me the greatest pleasure and peace of mind I've known," said Ben on the eve of the 1998 Masters. "Nothing I do in golf will ever be as meaningful as that event. I can't believe I was given the opportunity to win a tournament the week Harvey passed away, and, of all tournaments, the Masters, which I revere above all others, and to be remembered for having done so in his memory. All week, as I thought of Harvey, I tried to simplify my thoughts and just play the course as best I could."

Dave Marr, whose last years were spent as the golf analyst for NBC, made a comment over the air about his much younger friend, Crenshaw: "Week in and week out, Ben has broken more hearts than any golfer who's come along in forty years. We all root for him, the galleries root for him, heck, even some of the players root for him, and he just breaks your heart when he doesn't get the win." Well, on that warm April Sunday in Augusta, Crenshaw broke no hearts; he filled them—ours, the tournament patrons', the television viewers', his own, and the one that his kindly, silent partner, Harvey Penick, left behind.

'His Better Instincts'

❧≡◎ ○ ○ ○ ◎≡❧

In the early years of the Masters Tournament, it was the custom for Bob Jones, as the host, to be paired with the leader in the final round. This had a certain resonance with the press and public, who had taken Jones to their hearts and had expected him to demonstrate his mastery over the professionals. Alas, this was not to be. His matchless mental and emotional toughness had vanished, and, though no one knew it yet, his physical gifts were in decline.

Jones had not wanted to play in the first few tournaments, but had been talked into it by Clifford Roberts, Grantland Rice, and others who saw the obvious public relations value of his appearance in the fledgling event. Soon, though, Jones decided that he no longer wished to be a featured character in the drama, and sought a replacement to serve as a surrogate host in the final round, one that was still competitive and would not detract from the leader's glory.

His choice was Byron Nelson, who had won the Masters in 1937 and would win it again in 1942 in a bloodcurdling playoff with Ben Hogan. Nelson was then the fair-haired man of professional golf, more successful than Hogan or Snead, and seen as a more polished figure than either man. Byron's greatest years were ahead of him—as were Hogan's and Snead's—and Nelson fit the gentleman's role more naturally. Both Jones and Roberts would have weighed this factor rather carefully.

This practice began in 1938, and continued until 1956 when the leader after three rounds happened to be Ken Venturi, the sensational amateur. The trouble was, Venturi was a protege of Nelson's and had come to rely on Byron for coaching on the big occasions. Since no advantage or influence could be seen to be allowed by Jones, the game's greatest sportsman, a decision was reached to replace Nelson in the final pairing with a more neutral playing partner. The choice was Sam Snead, already winner of three Masters titles, and a great gallery favorite. More importantly, everyone knew that the last thing Snead could be accused of was coddling an opponent.

Venturi, of course, went on to a distinguished career in broadcasting and wound up as the coanchor for the Masters, as he still is, and for other tournaments covered by CBS. Twenty years later, in 1976, Raymond Floyd would enter the final round with an eight shot lead, and Venturi would be asked on television if he thought it possible that anyone could overcome such a lead. "Sure, it's conceivable," said Ken. "I know someone who lost an eight-shot lead in the Masters once. Matter of fact, I saw him in the mirror this morning while I was shaving."

Venturi, then an amateur wunderkind, shot 80 in that final round of 1956 and lost by one stroke to a tenacious Jack Burke, Jr., who made up eight strokes on the leader. "I hit every green on the front side, and shot 38," recalled Venturi. "On the day, I three-putted six times. No birdies and eight bogeys." He nearly won again in 1958, after turning pro, and finished second once more in 1960, a stroke behind Arnold Palmer, who closed with threes on the last three holes. "The following year, Arnold finished 4-4-6 to allow Gary Player to win by one shot. Sometimes you think, why me? But, that's the way it was," said Venturi.

Of the three close finishes, Venturi feels he had the best chance to win in 1956 while still an amateur. What would it have meant to him to be the first—and, to date, the only—amateur to win the Masters?

"I would have remained an amateur," said Venturi, without hesitation. "About a year later, I had dinner with Bobby Jones who told me that if I had won, he wanted me to take his place at the Masters. I was working for Ed Lowery at the time in his Ford dealership in San Francisco, and I guess I would have gone to work for Bill Ford in Detroit and served in some capacity under Jones and Cliff Roberts at Augusta National. I've never told this story to anyone before, but now I feel it can be told.

"During that dinner, Jones told me he always wanted to see an amateur win the Masters, and the idea that he would groom me as his amateur successor kind of grew out of that. But, if I had won and stayed amateur, I might not have won the U.S. Open in 1960. Life's funny that way. Jack Whitaker had the best line on life's twists: 'Fate has a way of bending the twig and fashioning a man to his better instincts.' As things have turned out, maybe I've been fashioned to my better instincts."

Tiger's Ascendance

-►═══○ ○ ○ ○ ═══◄-

No one had presumed to do to the Masters, or its legendary golf course, what Eldrick Woods did to it in 1997. Not Sarazen with his double-eagle, nor Snead with his three historic victories, nor Palmer with his four, not even Nicklaus with his six majestic wins had managed to turn the golf course on its ear quite the way young Woods did. Grizzled veterans quaked, grown men ran for cover, newsmen stood shaking their heads, and the rest of the world smiled.

Then, as the young man overcame a shaky start and burned a new record into the course, they cheered. His victory came in his first full season as a professional, but it was not his first Masters. He had played in two others as an amateur, indeed as the reigning United States Amateur Champion. In 1997, Woods was again the Amateur Champion, having won his third straight amateur title the previous summer in rather spectacular fashion by holing monster putts and routinely pulling victory from the jaws of defeat. Those comebacks were becoming a characteristic of his competitive performances.

Already he was living up to his nickname, Tiger, given to him by his father, Earl, in honor of a fellow combat veteran in Viet Nam. The great distances Woods achieved from the tee, already prodigious in his late teens, were becoming legend. But, he kept getting longer. By the time he played those first practice rounds at the Augusta National in 1997, Tiger Woods had virtually surpassed John Daly, the great seige gun of golf, as the longest hitter in the game.

After a shaky start in that first round, Woods tore the place apart. Paired with Nick Faldo on Thursday, he turned the front nine in 40, then shot the back in 30 to stand three strokes behind the leader, John Huston, who himself had holed a five-iron from the tenth fairway for an eagle, while playing the final hole, for his 67. Tiger's 66 on Friday moved him into the lead, and his 65 on Saturday put the tournament away. "Everybody's enamored of his long game—heck, we're all enamored of it," smiled Ben Crenshaw, "but he handled the little shots just beautifully and that set up his game and brought his confidence way up."

His closing 69 was little more than a formality, as he finished twelve strokes ahead of the runner-up, Tom Kite. The last man to humble a field this badly was Old Tom Morris, who had finished thirteen strokes ahead of Willie Park, Sr. in the British Open of 1862. That was 135 years ago, and Morris had only eight men to beat; Tiger was up against a field of 120 bloodthirsty mercenaries.

Kite was one of them, and he might have been excused for wondering what it takes to win a Masters. In twenty-four tries beginning in 1971, the tour's all-time leading money winner up to that point and its most dogged competitor, the fair-skinned Texan had finished second in three Masters and in the top five nine times. In fact, without Woods, Kite would have scored an exciting, one-stroke victory over a fast-closing Tommy Tolles, who finished with 67 in his maiden appearance at Augusta. Two strokes behind, alone in fourth, was a rejuvenated Tom Watson, and wouldn't that be an omen of things to come.

None of this mattered, of course. Tiger's performance obliterated everything. His power and skills were impressive, to be sure, but he was also a nineties cultural hero. His mixed racial background that three decades ago would have been a distinct liability in professional golf, was now a huge asset. People wanted to see representatives of minority groups win, and Tiger Woods knew how to do that. What's more, he knew how to do it in style.

If you were looking for drama, Tiger was your man. He could shoot 64s and 66s in final rounds to win tournaments. He could knock three-woods onto par-fives at the last hole and nearly win at places like Pebble Beach. He could roar back from nowhere and overtake a U.S. Open champion with 65 in the final round, and beat him on the second playoff hole.

In the Associated Press voting for sports story of 1997, Tiger's victory in the Masters beat out Mike Tyson's double-bite on Evander Holyfield's ears. Woods was named the AP's male athlete of the year, the first golfer to win the honor since Lee Trevino in 1971. The press, television, his agents, endorsement companies—even his father—were quick to claim a sort of mythical status for the young man. Hello, world.

The rush to anoint Tiger the next Nicklaus-Snead-Jones wrapped into one was led by Nicklaus himself, who proclaimed that Woods might well win as many Masters titles as had he and Palmer combined. Perhaps it was only the jab of a fading legend, but all of it taken together amounted to a stunning and finally tiresome display of hype and hope. The expectations grew by the week, by the month, and led inevitably to a much colder reality. Tiger would falter in the Open Championships of Britain and the United States, and produce a less than happy performance in the Ryder Cup that fall.

Before the 1998 Masters began, stories appeared in magazines that Woods would tear the scoring records to shreds unless the golf course were altered. Chairman Jack Stephens, presiding over his last Masters, told a press conference the club had declined to change the golf course for one man. What would the club do, the press persisted, if Tiger flattened the field again? In one of his better moments, Stephens replied gently: "I suppose we'll anoint him."

In the tournament, though, Tiger was unable to break 70 in any round and finished at 285 in a tie for eighth with three others. Two strokes ahead of him at 283 was the improbable Jack Nicklaus, who shot the last two rounds in 138, including a 68 on the last day. His playing partner, Ernie Els, said of Nicklaus: "I'm thirty years younger, and he beat me by four strokes. It's amazing how he plays great at the big moments." Woods did not need any reminders from the old master, but he got one in any case. On a happier note, Tiger then placed the green jacket on his friend, Mark O'Meara, who had holed a long birdie putt at the last to win his first major tournament.

As the century drew to a close, it was not at all clear whether Nicklaus's veiled challenge to Woods might be realized. The enormous speed Tiger generates in his swing produces stress that can be accommodated by a young body, but perhaps not as he matures. Indeed, there were signs of back troubles as the summer of 1998 wore on. Hello, Tiger. For all of his great power, though, Woods's greatest assets are a wonderful short game, an exceptional imagination, and a will to win. The petulance and impatience he has shown on occasion are the usual impulses of the young which a champion inevitably will discard. In all the hype, people tended to overlook the fact that when Woods came to defend his Masters title in 1998, he had yet to celebrate his twenty-second birthday.

Augusta National certainly favors the game Tiger plays. Anyone with a passing acquaintance of the place would be astonished if he didn't win more Masters tournaments, although the ten that Nicklaus suggested will not be so easy. Men as talented as Woods have discovered that there is more to this golf course, and to this fickle old game, than meets the eye.

A Tradition Returns

-+>===) o o o (===+-

A mong the appealing traditions that are on the wane at the
Masters is the presence of a strong amateur contingent.
This is partly due to the evolution of a sport in which its star
players remain amateurs only long enough to sign a rich professional contract, and sometimes not even that long. The last
time an amateur threw a scare into the pros in this spring classic
was the early 1960s when Charlie Coe was in his prime. Since
then, the amateur contingent has represented little more than
token participation in the Masters.

It must have grieved Bob Jones as he bore witness to this
gradual decline, although he was realist enough to see it coming
and to understand how implacable were the influences of money
and corporate involvement in golf. One can imagine his view-
ing the increasingly swollen purses and logoed golf apparel with
some distaste at the same time that he and his colleagues were
welcoming the effects of this growing fascination with golf for
the benefit of both the Masters Tournament and the Augusta
National Golf Club itself.

Jones was not so sentimental that he would want amateurs to

contend against form when their records gave little hint that they might, but he certainly would have been cheered when they did well, or, in the case of a Billy Joe Patton or Ken Venturi, nearly won it. That faint hope persists. After all, the Augusta National still reserves a part of the ceremony at the end of the tournament to honor the low amateur, a remnant of times past, perhaps, but nevertheless a nod to the great man who founded the tournament.

One of the things we seem to like about tradition is its pattern of renewal, even though it usually arrives in a new suit of clothes. It is this mantra that men like Palmer have taken up of late in defense of the old game, and that men like Jones wished to celebrate in the Masters. But this battered old tradition had been wearing out, and just when we thought it was dead, along came nineteen-year-old Matt Kuchar of Lake Mary, Florida. Kuchar, with his apple cheeks and wide grin, was the recently crowned United States Amateur Champion when he arrived in Augusta for the 1998 Masters. Nice young man, but no reason to take him seriously.

All he did was grab the heartstrings of the largest Masters gallery in history with a refreshing, eager optimism. Clearly, he was excited to be hitting wedge shots alongside the game's immortals, and just as clearly he was matching them. As it turns out, he's a player. All week long, people were wondering if Kuchar hadn't failed to acquire, along with his blissful composure and equally blissful putting stroke, a golfer's most precious possession, a frown. The youngster's smile was as broad as an Augusta fairway and as infectious as the azaleas that bloomed along the thirteenth hole. His was a storybook entrance into a storied event; if he frowned, it turns out, he would melt and be carried away in a pumpkin.

Neither Nicklaus in the fifties nor Woods in the nineties when making their first appearances in the Masters had struck such a chord in the galleries and with the millions watching on television. When he hit a good shot, Kuchar turned to the crowd a look of open-eyed wonder that reminded you of the little boy stepping out of the spacecraft in "Close Encounters of the Third Kind." When he hit a mediocre one, he managed a sheepish grin; a clunker elicited his strongest language: "Cornbread!" Or maybe, "Cheese and crackers!" He prefers to invent these mild expletives than resort to common profanity.

In this, he is unlike the man whose footsteps he has followed to Georgia Tech, where Matt is an undergraduate, to the U.S. Amateur title, and to the Masters. In style and elocution, too, Matt Kuchar and Bob Jones are different men, but in other ways alike. The manners, the gentle voice, the silky putting stroke, the lion's heart all seem similar in shape and origin; in any event, comparisons are being and likely will continue to be made.

"Bob Jones had great control of the pace of his swing, and so does young Kuchar. I never saw either one thrash at the ball," said Charles Yates, who was Jones's friend, fellow Atlantan and Georgia Tech man. Yates is the lone surviving amateur participant of that first Masters in 1934, and a member of the Augusta National. "Matt's performance in the 1998 Masters was magnificent, not only in the way he played but in the way he handled himself," Yates continued. "Matched against the best in the world, he has demonstrated the ability to pull himself together, and to me that's his most impressive quality. It indicates heart, and in that respect he reminds me of Jones. Like Jones, too, he has power when he wants it."

Prior to the Masters, Kuchar had been invited to play in the Bay Hill tournament in Orlando, an invitation that is offered each year by the host, Arnold Palmer, to the winner of the U.S. Amateur. Matt's father, Peter Kuchar, caddied for his son, and would do so again in the Masters and the other big tournaments that summer. "Matt played well and made the cut at Bay Hill," said Peter Kuchar. "That gave him the confidence he could play with those guys. If he doesn't play well there, I don't think he does nearly as well in the Masters."

The father and son team had four goals when they came to Augusta. Paired with Tiger Woods in the first round, the first goal was to make a respectable showing in front of the defending champion. The other goals were to make the cut, to finish as the low amateur, and to earn an invitation to return in 1999. The Georgia Tech golf team is invited to play Augusta National each year, so Matt was familiar with the course. His impressions? "It's heaven on earth, the most beautiful lawn you've ever seen," says Matt. "A round goes by faster than any you've ever played. You're sorry when each hole is gone."

Kuchar's game is built around his strengths: "Consistency and good course management are my strengths," said Matt. "I'm not the best ball striker, nor the best iron player, nor the best chipper, nor the best putter, but I know how to focus on the task at hand. That's what gets you to the next level." Not an exceptional putter? "Well, I do enjoy putting," he admits. Yes, we rather imagined so.

His tenacity was also evident, both in that Masters and in the U.S. Open that followed at the Olympic Club, in which Matt once again was low amateur and finished in the low twenty-four, earning an exemption into the 1999 renewal at Pinehurst. He held his own with Tiger Woods in the opening round Masters pairing, shooting 72 to Tiger's 71; then, paired in the first round at Olympic with U.S. Open champion Ernie Els and British Open champion Justin Leonard, Kuchar beat both men's scores.

His closing rounds of 68-72 in the 1998 Masters allowed Kuchar to finish at even par, tied for twenty-first place, which made the low twenty-four who were invited back for the 1999 Masters. All of their goals realized, Matt and his father attended the Sunday evening dinner given by the club's members to honor the winner each year. Kuchar and winner Mark O'Meara received standing ovations from "all the green jackets" and both players signed menus all during the dinner. Afterward, father and son went to the Crow's Nest, the little dormitory on the third floor of the clubhouse, to collect Matt's belongings.

"As we came down the stairs, we paused at the champions' locker room," recalled Peter Kuchar. "Since it was midnight and Matt hadn't turned into a pumpkin yet, we stayed there a moment just to soak up the feelings and the history of the room." Said Matt: "All of the Augusta National has an aura about it, but the champions' locker room is a special place. It speaks so much for the game of golf."

What of the comparisons with Jones? "That's the biggest compliment you could ever have," said Matt. "He was one of the finest gentlemen in golf." Perhaps there's another side to this, as well. There has been a resurgence of interest in Bobby Jones of late, due in part to the handsome biographies by Sid Matthew and others, in part to the red hot performances by the most recent amateur champions, Tiger Woods and Matt Kuchar. All of this has evoked the inevitable comparisons with Jones and drawn renewed attention to the founder of the Masters. "I believe there is a renaissance in amateur golf because of it," said Charles Yates.

Wouldn't that be something? As the century closes, the amateur spirit is renewed by, of all people, Bobby Jones, who again inspires the exploits of a couple of magnetic young players at, of all places, the Augusta National. And wouldn't that just bring a smile to the old legend's face?